Expectations of Excellence

CURRICULUM
STANDARDS
FOR
SOCIAL
STUDIES

Developed by
National Council for the Social Studies

NCSS

Task Force:

Donald Schneider, Chair
Susan A. Adler
R. Beery
Gloria Ladson-Billings
William R. Fernekes
Michael Hartoonian
Mary A. McFarland
Gerald Marker
Marjorie A. Montgomery
Pat Nickell
Corrinne Tevis

National Council for the Social Studies
8555 Sixteenth Street
Suite 500
Silver Spring, Maryland 20910
www.socialstudies.org

The Curriculum Standards for Social Studies were developed by a Task Force of the National Council for the Social Studies and approved by the NCSS Board of Directors in April 1994.

National Council for the Social Studies

President, 1991–92: Margit McGuire

President, 1992–93: Charlotte C. Anderson

President, 1993–94: Denny Schillings

President, 1994–95: Robert J. Stahl

President, 1995-96: H. Michael Hartoonian

President, 1996-97: Pat Nickell

President, 1997-98: Richard Diem

President, 1998-99: Tedd Levy

President, 1999-2000: Richard Theisen

President, 2000-2001: Susan Adler

President, 2001-2002: Adrian Davis

President, 2002-2003: Stephen Johnson

President, 2003-2004: Denee Mattioli

President, 2004-2005: Jesus Garcia

President, 2005-2006: Jeff Passe

President, 2006-2007: Peggy Altoff

Executive Director: Susan Griffin
Director of Publications: Michael Simpson
Director of Creative Services: Gene Cowan
Cover Design: Paul Wolski

Editorial services for this publication and writing of the executive summary provided by Lynn Page Whittaker of Scorpio Educational Communications, Alexandria, VA.

Library of Congress Catalog Card Number: 94-068635

ISBN 0-87986-065-0

Printed in the United States of America • Seventh printing, August 2006

10 9 8 7

Contents

EXECUTIVE SUMMARY

Thomas Jefferson, among others, emphasized that the vitality of a democracy depends upon the education and participation of its citizens. While such active civic participation includes becoming informed about issues and voting in elections, it can take many other diverse forms relating to the United States government, its history, its people, and its neighbors around the world. For example:

- Fannie Lou Hamer was an active citizen when she organized voter registration for Mississippi's black citizens during the civil rights movement of the 1960s.
- Ken Burns was an active citizen when he created the PBS series on the Civil War to demonstrate the dynamism and relevance of that period of U.S. history.
- High school students were active citizens when they convinced their school to switch from styrofoam to paper cups after conducting an environmental and cost analysis.
- And Senator Nancy Landon Kassebaum is an active citizen every day as she participates in committee discussions, votes on the Senate floor, speaks to community and school groups, listens to her constituents, and generally works within the political process to achieve her goals for this country.

All of these active citizens fulfill Jefferson's vision. But the United States and its democracy are constantly evolving and in continuous need of citizens who can adapt its enduring traditions and values to meet changing circumstances. Meeting that need is the mission of the social studies. In social studies, students develop a core of basic knowledge and ways of thinking drawn from many academic disciplines, learn how to analyze their own and others' opinions on important issues, and become motivated to participate in civic and community life as active, informed citizens.

The primary membership organization in the field, the National Council for the Social Studies (NCSS), has adopted this formal definition:

> Social studies is the integrated study of the social sciences and humanities to promote civic competence. Within the school program, social studies provides coordinated, systematic study drawing upon such disciplines as anthropology, archaeology, economics, geography, history, law, philosophy, political science, psychology, religion, and sociology, as well as appropriate content from the humanities, mathematics, and natural sciences. The primary purpose of social studies is to help young people develop the ability to make informed and reasoned decisions for the public good as citizens of a culturally diverse, democratic society in an interdependent world.

In essence, social studies promotes knowledge of and involvement in civic affairs. And because civic issues — such as health care, crime, and foreign policy — are multidisciplinary in nature, understanding these issues and developing resolutions to them require multidisciplinary education. These characteristics are the key defining aspects of social studies.

The Standards Process

The importance of social studies ensures that policymakers, educators, parents, and citizens of all kinds will want to know what students should be taught, how they will be taught, and how student achievement will be evaluated. The national curriculum standards in the social studies are designed to answer those questions. These standards, published in this book, define what students should be learning in social studies programs in the early grades, middle grades, and high school. To paraphrase a famous question, these standards specify what students should know and when they should know it.

The development of social studies standards has occurred concurrently with the development of standards in other areas of education (the arts, civics and government, economics, English, foreign language, geography, history, mathematics, physical education, science, and vocational education). The emphasis on education reform in the 1980s led to the National Governors Association's articulation of national educational goals in 1990 and the subsequent endorsement of those goals by the Bush administration. Congress then passed, in 1992, the Goals 2000: Educate America Act, codifying educational goals and sanctioning the development of national educational standards as a means of encouraging and evaluating student achievement. While that act included the disciplines named above, it omitted social studies. However, social studies educators, under the aegis of the NCSS, successfully annexed social studies to the national agenda and named a task force to develop curriculum standards.

The task force, chaired by Professor Don Schneider of the University of Georgia, a past president of NCSS, consisted of teachers from elementary, middle, and high school levels; university and college teacher educators; and state and school district social studies supervisors. The task force worked during 1993 and 1994 to develop the standards, review drafts, consider feedback from review panels, and revise and prepare the final document. The NCSS board of directors officially approved the standards document in April 1994. With the publishing of the standards in book form in fall 1994, NCSS begins dissemination of the standards to social studies educators around the country and launches a series of discussion and training workshops at conventions and in other venues at national, state, and district levels.

Organization and Use of the Standards

Because educational standards are being developed both in social studies and in many of the individual disciplines that contribute to social studies, one might ask: what is the relationship among these various sets of standards? The answer is that the social studies standards address overall curriculum design and comprehensive student performance expectations, while the individual discipline standards (civics and government, economics, geography, and history) provide focused and enhanced content detail. Teachers and curriculum designers are encouraged first to establish their program frameworks using the social studies standards as a guide, and then to use the standards from history, geography, civics, economics, and others to guide the development of grade level strands and courses. Using all of these standards in concert with one another allows educators to give adequate attention to both integrated and single discipline configurations.

A metaphor helps to illustrate the relationship between social studies and specific individual disciplines. Consider a musical ensemble such as an orchestra (the social studies program) as it performs a specific musical composition (a grade level or specific course within the curriculum). At certain times, one instrument (a discipline such as history) takes the lead while others (such as geography and economics) play supporting roles. At other times, several instruments (history, geography, economics) play together on an equal basis to explore the composer's thematic aims. The quality of the performance is the result of the composer's writing of the music (design of the social studies curriculum), the unique qualities of individual instruments (the contribution of individual disciplines), the acoustics of the setting (expertise of curriculum planners and teachers, school site facilities, and instructional resources), and the skills of musicians and the conductor (the abilities of students, teachers, and program planners).

These social studies standards are thus organized to incorporate learning experiences from many disciplines. This book presenting the social studies standards is designed to serve three purposes:

1. to serve as a framework for social studies program design from kindergarten through grade 12 (K–12);
2. to function as a guide for curriculum decisions by providing student performance expectations in the areas of knowledge, processes, and attitudes; and
3. to provide examples of classroom activities that will guide teachers as they design instruction to help their students meet performance expectations.

The framework of the standards consists of ten themes incorporating fields of study that roughly correspond with one or more relevant disciplines. The first theme, "Culture," for instance, includes elements of anthropology, geography, history, and sociology. These ten themes span the educational levels from early to middle grades to high school. The standards are expressed in statements that begin "Social studies programs should include experiences that provide for the study of" — for instance, Culture. Student performance expectations within that theme are then specified, and examples of classroom activities are provided as illustrations of how to design learning experiences to help students meet the performance expectations.

The Ten Themes

The ten themes that form the framework of the social studies standards are:

Culture. The study of culture prepares students to answer questions such as: What are the common characteristics of different cultures? How do belief systems, such as religion or political ideals, influence other parts of the culture? How does the culture change to accommodate different ideas and beliefs? What does language tell us about the culture? In schools, this theme typically appears in units and courses dealing with geography, history, sociology, and anthropology, as well as multicultural topics across the curriculum.

Time, Continuity, and Change. Human beings seek to understand their historical roots and to locate themselves in time. Knowing how to read and reconstruct the past allows one to develop a historical perspective and to answer questions such as: Who am I? What happened in the past? How am I connected to those in the past? How has the world changed and how might it change in the future? Why does our personal sense of relatedness to the past change? This theme typically appears in courses in history and others that draw upon historical knowledge and habits.

People, Places, and Environments. The study of people, places, and human-environment interactions assists students as they create their spatial views and geographic perspectives of the world beyond their personal locations. Students need the knowledge, skills, and understanding to answer questions such as: Where are things located? Why are they located where they are? What do we mean by "region"? How do landforms change? What implications do these changes have for people? In schools, this theme typically appears in units and courses dealing with area studies and geography.

Individual Development and Identity. Personal identity is shaped by one's culture, by groups, and by institutional influences. Students should consider such questions as: How do people learn? Why do people behave as they do? What influences how people learn, perceive, and grow? How do people meet their basic needs in a variety of contexts? How do individuals develop from youth to adulthood? In schools, this theme typically appears in units and courses dealing with psychology and anthropology.

Individuals, Groups, and Institutions. Institutions such as schools, churches, families, government agencies, and the courts play an integral role in people's lives. It is important that students learn how institutions are formed, what controls and influences them, how they influence individuals and culture, and how they are maintained or changed. Students may address questions such as: What is the role of institutions in this and other societies? How am I influenced by institutions? How do institutions change? What is my role in institutional change? In schools this theme typically appears in units and courses dealing with sociology, anthropology, psychology, political science, and history.

Power, Authority, and Governance. Understanding the historical development of structures of power, authority, and governance and their evolving functions in contemporary U.S. society and other parts of the world is essential for developing civic competence. In exploring this theme, students confront questions such as: What is power? What forms does it take? Who holds it? How is it gained, used, and justified? What is legitimate authority? How are governments created, structured, maintained, and changed? How can individual rights be protected within the context of majority rule? In schools, this theme typically appears in units and courses dealing with government, politics, political science, history, law, and other social sciences.

Production, Distribution, and Consumption. Because people have wants that often exceed the resources available to them, a variety of ways have evolved to answer such questions as: What is to be produced? How is production to be organized? How are goods and services to be distributed? What is the most effective allocation of the factors of production (land, labor, capital, and management)? In schools, this theme typically appears in units and courses dealing with economic concepts and issues.

Science, Technology, and Society. Modern life as we know it would be impossible without technology and the science that supports it. But technology brings with it many questions: Is new technology always better than old? What can we learn from the past about how new technologies result in broader social change, some of which is unanticipated? How can we cope with the ever-increasing pace of change? How can we manage technology so that the greatest number of people benefit from it? How can we preserve our fundamental values and beliefs in the midst of technological change? This theme draws upon the natural and physical sciences, social sciences, and the humanities, and appears in a variety of social studies courses, including history, geography, economics, civics, and government.

Global Connections. The realities of global interdependence require understanding the increasingly important and diverse global connections among world societies and the frequent tension between national interests and global priorities. Students will need to be able to address such international issues as health care, the environment, human rights, economic competition and interdependence, age-old ethnic enmities, and political and military alliances. This theme typically appears in units or courses dealing with geography, culture, and economics, but may also draw upon the natural and physical sciences and the humanities.

Civic Ideals and Practices. An understanding of civic ideals and practices of citizenship is critical to full participation in society and is a central purpose of the social studies. Students confront such questions as: What is civic participation and how can I be involved? How has the meaning of citizenship evolved? What is the balance between rights and responsibilities? What is the role of the citizen in the community and the nation, and as a member of the world community? How can I make a positive difference? In schools, this theme typically appears in units or courses dealing with history, political science, cultural anthropology, and fields such as global studies, law-related education, and the humanities.

This book includes one chapter each for the early grades, the middle grades, and the high school level. Within those chapters, each theme is followed by a list of student performance expectations and classroom activities. To illustrate how the standards are applied using the themes and performance expectations, the following three sections provide examples from the early grades, middle grades, and high school.

An Example from the Early Grades

For instance, take the theme "Culture." For the early grades, the standard (stated first, in a sentence) and its performance expectations (listed in alphabetical order) are as follows:

Social studies programs should include experiences that provide for the study of *culture and cultural diversity,* so that the learner can:

   a. explore and describe similarities and differences in the ways groups, societies, and cultures address similar human needs and concerns;

   b. give examples of how experiences may be interpreted differently by people from diverse cultural perspectives and frames of reference;

   c. describe ways in which language, stories, folktales, music, and artistic creations serve as expressions of culture and influence behavior of people living in a particular culture;

   d. compare ways in which people from different cultures think about and deal with their physical environment and social conditions;

   e. give examples and describe the importance of cultural unity and diversity within and across groups.

One of the classroom activities describes the experiences of a teacher, Carlene Jackson, who uses a new program to develop geographic understanding in her first grade class. Before the first day of school, Jackson looks over her class list, inferring that she will have students of Mexican, Vietnamese, and Korean ancestry, as well as of African-American and European-American backgrounds. Jackson and her students decide to study how families meet their basic needs of food, clothing, and shelter in five places: their community; Juarez, Mexico; Hanoi, Vietnam; Lagos, Nigeria; and Frankfurt, Germany. The class reads books and stories, looks at photos and slides, watches videos, and talks to speakers from their cities. Students sharpen their reading, writing, and speaking skills and learn new geography skills such as map reading. For each city, they read and discuss something about its location, climate, region, and people. This activity is designed to address performance expectations a, b, and d.

An Example from the Middle Grades

At this level, the theme of "Culture" involves the following standard of performance expectations. Note how they build on the expectations from the lower grades:

Social studies programs should include experiences that provide for the study of *culture and cultural diversity*, so that the learner can:
   a. compare similarities and differences in the ways groups, societies, and cultures meet human needs and concerns;
   b. explain how information and experiences may be interpreted by people from diverse cultural perspectives and frames of reference;
   c. explain and give examples of how language, literature, the arts, architecture, other artifacts, traditions, beliefs, values, and behaviors contribute to the development and transmission of culture;
   d. explain why individuals and groups respond differently to their physical and social environments and/or changes to them on the basis of shared assumptions, values, and beliefs;
   e. articulate the implications of cultural diversity, as well as cohesion, within and across groups.

One of the accompanying classroom activities describes John Parker's seventh grade world studies unit on Australia. Student groups use maps to identify physical and cultural patterns in Australia today and hypothesize that people live the way that they do because the natural-physical environment (resources, climate, terrain) requires them to in order to survive. After sharing their hypotheses, some students turn to their textbook chapter on Australia to find information to prove or disprove their hypotheses; others consult more sophisticated reference sources; others use picture books to add visual evidence.

Groups revise their hypotheses on the basis of their findings and then view a relevant video. Parker then asks students to contrast their hypothesis that people live the way they do in Australia because of the physical-natural environment with the fact that the aboriginal people who were there when the Europeans arrived live in such a different way in the same natural environment. Student groups develop and share cultural explanations to account for these differences. Some emphasize belief systems; others, learned behavior patterns. After the discussion, each student writes a paragraph presenting his or her explanation for the difference in the ways of contemporary Australians and aboriginal peoples. This activity is designed to address performance expectations a, b, c, d, and e.

An Example from the High School Level

At this level, the performance expectations for the theme of "Culture" are as follows. Note again how they build on those of the previous level:

Social studies programs should include experiences that provide for the study of *culture and cultural diversity*, so that the learner can:

a. analyze and explain the ways groups, societies, and cultures address human needs and concerns;

b. predict how data and experiences may be interpreted by people from diverse cultural perspectives and frames of reference;

c. apply an understanding of culture as an integrated whole that explains the functions and interactions of language, literature, the arts, traditions, beliefs and values, and behavior patterns;

d. compare and analyze societal patterns for preserving and transmitting culture while adapting to environmental or social change;

e. demonstrate the value of cultural diversity, as well as cohesion, within and across groups;

f. interpret patterns of behavior reflecting values and attitudes that contribute or pose obstacles to cross-cultural understanding;

g. construct reasoned judgments about specific cultural responses to persistent human issues;

h. explain and apply ideas, theories, and modes of inquiry drawn from anthropology and sociology in the examination of persistent issues and social problems.

One of the activity examples involves a unit on prayer in schools. In the opening discussion in teacher Bill Tate's class, one student favors prayer in school, noting that "every important document of this country makes reference to God, and when presidents or judges are sworn in, they place their hands on the Bible." Another student responds that she is Buddhist, so her concept of God and religion is different from what the first student was talking about. A Muslim student points out that Islam is the fastest growing religion in the world, and asks: "What if Muslims become a religious majority in the U.S.? Which American principle would prevail — majority rule or freedom of religion?" Another chimes in her opinion that freedom of religion really means freedom from a state-imposed religion. She points out that the United States is a democracy not a theocracy, and argues that even though God is mentioned in U.S. documents and certain ceremonies, public schools should not sanction any one form of religion.

Tate records students' comments on the board, ensuring that everyone is heard and no one's ideas are ridiculed. As the period ends, he presents a case study about a city's decision to place a nativity scene on public property. For homework and discussion the next day, students are to determine whether they agree or disagree with the decision, list reasons supporting their opinion, and research analogous historical or contemporary situations. This activity is designed to address performance expectations b, c, e, and f.

Conclusion: Meeting the Challenge

The United States and its democratic system of government are constantly evolving. No one can predict with certainty what may be needed from its citizens to preserve and protect it fifty years from now. For social studies to perform its mission of promoting civic competence, students must learn not only a body of knowledge but how to think and how to be flexible in using many resources to resolve civic issues. It is not overstating the case to say that America's future depends on it.

These national curriculum standards for social studies represent educators' best thinking about what is needed to educate future citizens to meet that challenge.

Foreword

In 1992, the Board of Directors of the National Council for the Social Studies created a Task Force on Standards for Social Studies in order to ensure that, in the "era of standards," an integrated social science, behavioral science, and humanities approach for achieving academic and civic competence was available to guide social studies decisionmakers in K-12 schools in the United States.

This document, the product of that task force, contains a set of curriculum standards to guide social studies curricula, teaching, learning tasks, and assessment. These standards are recommended for use in assessing the quality and extent of social studies curricula and student achievement, including the long-term retention and maintenance of targeted content, skills, attitudes, and perspectives aligned with these standards. They also can be used as a template against which existing curricula as well as proposed curricula can be analyzed and assessed.

These standards do not represent a set of mandated outcomes or establish a national curriculum for the social studies. Rather, they should be used as guides and criteria to establish integrated state, district, school, department, and classroom curriculum plans to guide instruction, learning, and assessment. Except for clustering the standards into early grades, middle grades, and high school sets, no scope and sequence that must be followed or subject matter content that must be taught are listed. Decisions such as scope, specific content, and sequence are in the hands of those who are seeking to improve their social studies curricula to increase the quality of their students' social studies knowledge and skills. These state and local decisions will augment and enhance the framework these national standards provide.

These standards were developed and organized in full collaboration with social studies educators in the field, scholars in the academic disciplines, and the general public. Thousands of copies were distributed by mail; at workshops on the state, regional, and national levels; and through direct contact with thousands of teachers, content specialists, teacher educators, curriculum specialists, and supervisors as well as members of the general public and other educational organizations. Major revisions were made because of the valuable input of these individuals and groups. Both the standards and this document are clearer, stronger, and more practical as a result of the process that was followed and the feedback that was received. In a very real sense, both are the product of social studies educators, mostly classroom teachers, collaborating to improve and enhance, not just reform, social studies education. The members of the task force and the Officers and Board of the National Council for the Social Studies thank all of those who contributed during this constructive, consensus-building process.

Educators on all levels, including pre-service and in-service teacher educators, attempting to develop curriculum to achieve desired results regarding student knowledge, skills, attitudes, and perspectives, will find these standards useful because they suggest priorities, a set of fundamental themes, and student performance expectations that are essential to a sound social studies curriculum.

A social studies perspective is academically sound, multidisciplinary, and integrative. The leadership of the social studies profession envisions these standards to serve as a framework within which educators and content experts in the separate social sciences, behavioral sciences, and humanities should feel comfortable. We perceive these standards to be inclusionary rather than exclusionary of these disciplines. Social studies educators can certainly augment and enhance this framework by drawing key concepts, content, and methods of inquiry from all the individual disciplines. To be more empowering, these should be incorporated into the curriculum, instructional activities, and assessment in an integrative rather than single-discipline manner.

These standards provide a solid foundation upon which major reform of what goes on in schools can be based. In that way, we can give our young people a solid integrated academic background for living in both today's and tomorrow's worlds. Given that the focus of the social studies includes civic competence, the expectation is that quality implementation of these standards will improve the quality of each student's life both as an individual and as a member of the many social communities within which each lives.

Finally, implementation of these standards will require a cooperative effort and commitment. Political leaders and school boards with public support will need to provide adequate resources, incentives, and school settings for teachers and students. Teachers will have the ultimate responsibility for implementing the standards within the context of their local settings and student populations. The task—the challenge— is to realize that to prepare individuals and citizens for tomorrow's world requires a vision of the social studies and of social studies education that can make a qualitative difference in students' thinking and acting and the implementation of a curriculum framework aligned with what they need. This document reflects such a vision and provides such a framework.

Robert J. Stahl
President, 1994–95
National Council for the Social Studies

Preface

As Ben Franklin was leaving the constitutional convention one afternoon in September 1787, a young woman approached him and asked, "Well, Dr. Franklin, what have you given us?"

"A republic—if you can keep it" was his reply.

Keeping the republic requires that United States citizens labor vigilantly to ensure that this form of government continues to extend the blessings of liberty to all its citizens.

As we move toward the twenty-first century, it is clear that the dominant social, economic, cultural, and scientific trends that have defined the western world for five centuries are rapidly leading in new directions. We are living in a time colored by dramatic change not unlike the transformations associated with the beginning of the fifteenth century that brought new conceptions of time, community, family, and even nationhood. We are also being forced to redefine our fundamental institutions and to construct new social contexts and relationships as we continue efforts to form a more perfect union, establish justice, ensure domestic tranquillity, provide for the common defense, promote the general welfare, and secure the blessings of liberty to ourselves and our children.

The twenty-first century will bring us face to face with the information-electronic-biotechnological age. New issues, together with old problems, will confront us and tax our intellectual and moral fiber, making it increasingly difficult to implement the goals that define us as a nation. Demographic and statistical data force us to look closely at the changing nature of our families, the reconceptualization of work, the distribution of justice and poverty, the conditions of illiteracy, and the age, class, gender, and ethnic makeup of our people. The world is diverse, ethically challenged, yet globally interdependent, and the task of "bringing the blessing of the American dream to all" calls for citizens with a new sense of purpose.

Given the realities of today's world and the desire of U.S. citizens to carry the ideals of our republic into the future, it is necessary that we create a new vision for our work as social studies educators. That vision must motivate us toward a commitment to extend the promise of full scholarship and citizenship to each and every person in the United States. The central focus of this goal is the design and implementation of social studies education as a liberating force in the life of every citizen. That is, our work should illuminate the essential connection among social studies learning, democratic values, and positive citizenship.

As a people, then, our first priority, our first public policy goal, must be to ensure our survival as a free nation through the development of students who can assume the office of citizen. What expectations should we have of students who are to assume this office? The vision of the members of the National Council for the Social Studies (NCSS) Curriculum Standards Task Force is the following:

> The informed social studies student understands and applies to personal and public experiences the content perspectives of the several academic fields of the social studies. Equally important, the informed

social studies student exhibits the habits of mind and behavior of one who respects the relationship between education (i.e., learning) and his or her responsibility to promote the common good.

To achieve such a vision of social studies, we must ensure that students become intimately acquainted with scholarship, artisanship, leadership, and citizenship. These mutually inclusive attributes are the hallmarks of excellence in social studies—a program in which students will gain the necessary knowledge, skills, and attitudes to understand, respect, and practice the ways of the scholar, the artisan, the leader, and the citizen.

Our "we the people" republic is built upon the principle that the people occupy an important position in government—the office of citizen; thus, it is necessary that attention be paid to the education of those who assume this office. The civic culture of our nation is built upon four components: the legislative, the executive, the judicial, and the people. The three branches of government depend on the people (the fourth branch), who must develop the attributes of the enlightened citizen—i.e., individuals who understand the rights and responsibilities of citizenship.

Citizens who take this office seriously are in touch with the cultural heritage of the nation. They possess knowledge of the economic, political, and social factors that make up the human ecosystem in which all must function, and they understand its relationship to natural systems. They understand the principles of rule of law, legal limits to freedom, and majority rule with protection for minority rights. They have informed spatial, temporal, and cultural perspectives. They possess the attitudes and behaviors that support fair play and cooperation. Without a conscious effort to teach these ideals, a free republic will not long endure.

As Maya Angelou bid us on Inauguration Day 1993:

> "Lift up your eyes upon
> This day breaking for you.
> Give birth again
> to the dream."

—Michael Hartoonian
for the members of the Curriculum Standards Task Force

One INTRODUCTION

Introduction   **What Is Social Studies?**

In 1992, the Board of Directors of the National Council for the Social Studies, the primary membership organization for social studies educators, adopted the following definition:

> Social studies is the integrated study of the social sciences and humanities to promote civic competence. Within the school program, social studies provides coordinated, systematic study drawing upon such disciplines as anthropology, archaeology, economics, geography, history, law, philosophy, political science, psychology, religion, and sociology, as well as appropriate content from the humanities, mathematics, and natural sciences. The primary purpose of social studies is to help young people develop the ability to make informed and reasoned decisions for the public good as citizens of a culturally diverse, democratic society in an interdependent world.

Social studies is taught in kindergarten through grade 12 in schools across the nation. As a field of study, social studies may be more difficult to define than is a single discipline such as history or geography, precisely because it is multidisciplinary and interdisciplinary and because it is sometimes taught in one class (perhaps called "social studies") and sometimes in separate discipline-based classes within a department of social studies.

Two main characteristics, however, distinguish social studies as a field of study: it is designed to promote civic competence; and it is integrative, incorporating many fields of endeavor. In specific and more detailed terms, these distinctions mean the following:

1. *Social studies programs have as a major purpose the promotion of civic competence—which is the knowledge, skills, and attitudes required of students to be able to assume "the office of citizen" (as Thomas Jefferson called it) in our democratic republic.* Although civic competence is not the only responsibility of social studies nor is it exclusive to the field, it is more central to social studies than any other subject area in the schools.

The National Council for the Social Studies (NCSS) has long supported civic competence as the goal of social studies. By doing so, NCSS has recognized the importance of educating students who are committed to the ideas and values of our democratic republic and who are able to use knowledge about their community, nation, and world, along with skills of data collection and analysis, collaboration, decision-making, and problem-solving. Students who have these commitments, knowledge, and skills will be the most capable of shaping our future and sustaining and improving our democracy.

2. *K–12 social studies programs integrate knowledge, skills, and attitudes within and across disciplines.* Integrated social studies programs across the nation take many forms, varying in the amount and form of disciplinary integration:

- At *primary levels,* children often learn social studies through learning opportunities that are highly integrated across several disciplines. These often take the form of units constructed around themes. For example, teachers using the theme "time, continuity, and change" would likely engage young learners in studies using history, science, and language arts.

- As students proceed to *middle and higher levels,* social studies programs may continue to be highly integrated and in some cases planned by interdisciplinary teams of teachers (for example, social studies, science, mathematics, humanities). Alternatively, programs may be planned as interdisciplinary courses or more exclusively linked to specific disciplines (for example, a history course that also draws from geography, economics, political science).

3. *Social studies programs help students construct a knowledge base and attitudes drawn from academic disciplines as specialized ways of viewing reality.* Each discipline begins from a specific perspective and applies unique "processes for knowing" to the study of reality. History, for instance, uses the perspective of time to explore causes and effects of events in the past. Political science, on the other hand, uses the perspective of political institutions to explore structures and processes of governing.

It is important for students in social studies programs to begin to understand, appreciate, and apply knowledge, processes, and attitudes from academic disciplines. But even such discipline-based learning draws simultaneously from several disciplines in clarifying specific concepts. A study of the concept of "the common good," for example, may draw upon some or all of the following:

- the discipline of *history,* to determine the concept's origin, study primary source documents that define and address the concept, and analyze the concept's development over time;
- the discipline of *geography,* to locate where the concept was first developed, map its movement from one continent or nation to another, and recognize the power of the diffusion of ideas as an example of global linkage;
- the discipline of *political science,* to determine the developing meaning of the concept as it is promoted or limited through existing political institutions, to study examples of actual practice related to the common good, and to acknowledge the need for citizen involvement in closing the distance between the ideal and reality;
- the discipline of *sociology,* to examine the role of individuals, groups, and institutions and their relationship and responsibility to the common good, and to develop an understanding of the complexities of those relationships resulting from the diversity of beliefs, values, and structures within and among them; and
- communication abilities from *language arts/English* and the *fine arts* to enable students to express their understanding of the concept in a personally meaningful way.

The example could be extended to other disciplines, but the point is that discipline-based knowledge, processes, and attitudes are fully utilized within social studies programs. Students in social studies programs must study the development of social phenomena and concepts over time; must have a sense of place and interrelationships among places across time and space; must understand institutions and processes that define our democratic republic; must draw from other disciplines appropriate to a more complete understanding of an idea or phenomenon; and must experience concepts reflectively and actively, through reading, thinking, discussing, and writing.

4. *Social studies programs reflect the changing nature of knowledge, fostering entirely new and highly integrated approaches to resolving issues of significance to humanity.* Over the last fifty years, the scholarly community has begun to rethink disciplinary boundaries and encourage more integration across disciplines. This process has been spurred by pressures such as the following:

- Social issues, such as poverty, crime, and public health, are increasingly understood to transcend the boundaries of disciplines, cultures, and nations. As these issues grow increasingly complex, the work to develop solutions demands an increasingly integrated view of scholarly domains and of the world itself.

- Many scholars now define themselves by the issues and problems they address and use several disciplines to inform their work. Entirely new departments and programs reflect this development. Academic programs in American Studies, African-American Studies, Biotechnology, and Medical Ethics, for example, draw on multiple disciplines and their processes to address the needs of humanity.

- Technology provides increasingly easy access to data bases that are cross-disciplinary and multidisciplinary as well as to scholarship in many disciplines.

- Scholars increasingly consider themselves to be members of the international academic community and share findings regularly across intellectual and geographic boundaries.

The more accurately the K–12 social studies program addresses the contemporary conditions of real life and of academic scholarship, the more likely such a program is to help students develop a deeper understanding of how to know, how to apply what they know, and how to participate in building a future.

It is within this context that these social studies standards were created. They pay attention to the specific contributions of history, the social sciences, humanities, fine arts, the natural sciences, and other disciplines, while simultaneously providing an umbrella for the integrative potential of these several disciplines. This characteristic is the nature and strength of social studies: recognizing the importance of the disciplines and their specific perspectives in understanding topics, issues, and problems, but also recognizing that topics, issues, and problems transcend the boundaries of single disciplines and demand the power of integration within and across them.

How Do We Achieve Excellence in Social Studies?

To achieve the vision of social studies, we must ensure that students become intimately acquainted with scholarship, artisanship, leadership, and citizenship. Excellence in social studies will be achieved by programs in which students gain the knowledge, skills, and attitudes necessary to understand, respect, and practice the ways of the scholar, the artisan, the leader, and the citizen in support of the common good.

Supporting the Common Good

As citizens of a democracy, we support one of our republic's most important ideals: the common good, i.e., the general welfare of all individuals and groups within the community.

The common good is supported when all citizens become aware that the meaning and purpose of education in a democratic republic is the intellectual and ethical development of "student-citizens," young people who will soon assume the role of citizen. Individuals must understand that their self-interest is dependent upon the well-being of others in the community. Attention to the common good means putting first things first. If educators address the ethical and intellectual habits of students, other priorities will be realized.

Our moral imperative as educators is to see all children as precious and recognize that they will inherit a world of baffling complexity. Our responsibility is to respect and support the dignity of the individual, the health of the community, and the common good of all. This responsibility demands that we teach our students to recognize and respect the diversity that exists within the community.

Adopting Common and Multiple Perspectives

Each person experiences life in an individual way, responding to the world from a very personal perspective. People also share common perspectives as members of groups, communities, societies, and nations—that is, as part of a dynamic world community. A well-designed social studies curriculum will help each learner construct a blend of personal, academic, pluralist, and global views of the human condition in the following ways:

- Students should be helped to construct a *personal perspective* that enables them to explore emerging events and persistent or recurring issues, considering implications for self, family, and the whole national and world community. Social studies students need to learn to make choices after weighing their personal expectations, along with the pros, cons, responsibilities, and consequences of those choices for themselves and others.

- Students should be helped to construct an *academic perspective* through study and application of social studies learning experiences. The social studies disciplines provide specific points of view. Discipline-based concepts such as "democratic republic," "citizen," "common good," and others help learners construct the meaning of ideals U.S. citizens hold in common. Discipline-based concepts such as "class," "race," "equal access," and others help learners ask how to live in communities characterized by both unity and diversity and how to close the gap between ideals and reality. The informed social studies learner applies knowledge and processes from academic disciplines and from interdisciplinary means to both personal and social experiences.

- Students should be helped to construct a *pluralist perspective* based on diversity. This perspective involves respect for differences of opinion and preference; of race, religion, and gender; of class and ethnicity; and of culture in general. This construction should be based on the realization that differences exist among individuals and the conviction that this diversity can be positive and socially enriching. Students need to learn that the existence of cultural and philosophical differences are not "problems" to be solved; rather, they are healthy and desirable qualities of democratic community life.

- Students should be helped to construct a *global perspective* that includes knowledge, skills, and commitments needed to live wisely in a world that possesses limited resources and that is characterized by cultural diversity. A global perspective involves viewing the world and its people with understanding and concern. This perspective develops a sense of responsibility for the needs of all people and a commitment to finding just and peaceful solutions to global problems.

Personal, academic, pluralist, and global perspectives all develop within the framework of civic responsibility that is the hallmark of the democratic national culture committed to individual liberty and the common good. These interrelated perspectives will be developed in a social studies curriculum designed to enable students to use knowledge in the following ways: to conceptualize contexts of issues or phenomena; to consider causality; to inquire about the validity of explanations; and to create new explanations and models for grappling with persistent and/or recurring issues across time, space, and cultures.

Applying Knowledge, Skills, and Values to Civic Action

It is important that students become able to connect knowledge, skills, and values to civic action as they engage in social inquiry.

Knowledge

Knowledge is constructed by learners as they attempt to fit new information, experiences, feelings, and relationships into their existing or emerging intellectual, aesthetic, and emotional constructs. Disciplinary or specialized knowledge is useful but not always sufficient for developing contextual understanding of the phenomena we seek to comprehend. In these instances, ideas, principles, concepts, and information from a number of fields may be relevant to the topic studied. In the social studies, therefore, educators draw widely from a number of disciplines to construct curricular experiences enabling students to actively relate new knowledge to existing understanding.

If we want our students to be better thinkers and better decision-makers, they must have contact with those accustomed to thinking with precision, refinement, and clarity. We must encourage them to be critical and copious readers of the best media, print, audio, and video content, writers of reflective essays, and critics of social phenomena. An awareness of the relationship among social studies content, skills, and learning context can help us establish criteria for developing reflective social inquiry. This disposition toward reflective thinking is essential if we wish to foster democratic thought and action.

Skills

The skills that should be promoted in an excellent social studies program include the following:
- — acquiring information and manipulating data;
- — developing and presenting policies, arguments, and stories;

— constructing new knowledge; and

— participating in groups.

These skill categories should not be seen as a fragmented list of things that students and teachers should do. Rather, they should be used as an interconnected framework in which each skill is dependent upon and enriched by all other skills. All together are necessary for a program of excellence:

Acquiring information and manipulating data. To develop this skill category, the social studies program should be designed to increase the student's ability to read, study, search for information, use social science technical vocabulary and methods, and use computers and other electronic media.

Developing and presenting policies, arguments, and stories. To develop this skill category, the social studies program should be designed to increase the student's ability to use the writing process and to classify, interpret, analyze, summarize, evaluate, and present information in well-reasoned ways that support better decision-making for both individuals and society.

Constructing new knowledge. To develop this skill category, the social studies program should be designed to increase the student's ability to conceptualize unfamiliar categories of information, establish cause/effect relationships, determine the validity of information and arguments, and develop a new story, model, narrative, picture, or chart that adds to the student's understanding of an event, idea, or persons while meeting criteria of valid social studies research.

Participating in groups. To develop this skill category, the social studies program should be designed to increase the student's ability to express and advocate reasoned personal convictions within groups, recognize mutual ethical responsibility in groups, participate in negotiating conflicts and differences or maintain an individual position because of its ethical basis, work individually and in groups, and accept and fulfill responsibilities associated with citizenship in a democratic republic. (See Appendix A. Essential Skills for Social Studies for additional details on necessary skills.)

Values

Some values are so central to our way of life and view of the common good that we need to develop student commitment to them through systematic social studies experiences. These include such fundamental rights as the right to life, liberty, individual dignity, equality of opportunity, justice, privacy, security, and ownership of private property. They include as well the basic freedoms of worship, thought, conscience, expression, inquiry, assembly, and participation in the political process. In some instances, the social studies curriculum will focus on how values are formed and how they influence human behavior rather than on building commitment to specific values. In other instances, the emphasis will be placed upon helping students weigh priorities in situations in which a conflict exists between or among desirable values (i.e., those that form our common beliefs about rights, freedoms, and responsibilities of human beings in a democratic society). (See Appendix B. Democratic Beliefs and Values for the complete list.)

Introduction

Democratic societies are characterized by hard choices. Many choices involve personal behavior; for example, should I vacation in a state that has just passed a law of which I disapprove? In a democratic society, many choices involve whether to support people or groups who advocate certain public policies. Choices become dilemmas when they involve issues that pit our most cherished values against each other. For example, we value business competition and believe that consumers should decide what survives in the marketplace, but we also believe that the public should be protected from unsafe products. Because we value human life, we vote for legislators who support helmet and seat-belt laws, but we also believe that people should control their own lives. Social studies should not dictate to students what the solutions should be to such dilemmas, but it should teach them how to analyze and discuss those dilemmas within the context of the civil discourse required to maintain a democratic society.

Sometimes the choices confronting citizens are extremely difficult, and decisions may lead to actions that require personal sacrifice—even at the risk of personal well-being or life. We generally value law-abiding behavior, for example, but we also recognize that there are times when laws represent something so wrong that they must be broken. The civil rights movement in the 1960s involved just such a dilemma, as did the choice in the eighteenth century between obeying British laws or supporting the American Revolution.

Social studies can help students search for situations analogous to these issues in both contemporary and historical settings. By learning ways others have responded to such dilemmas, students can begin to understand that choices they or their society face have been confronted by others in different times and places. By helping students learn how to understand ideals such as patriotism and loyalty and to examine the meaning of justice, equality, and privacy in specific dilemma situations, educators can give them practice in discussing the arguments and evidence that surround such dilemmas. By guiding them to clarify the facts connected with value dilemmas and teaching them how to identify pros, cons, and consequences of various positions, educators can also give students tools that will inform their decision-making processes as they face difficult choices in life.

Although there is no finite list of persistent issues and dilemmas in social studies, the following are typical of those with which people have wrestled over time. They are often stated as one value versus another because that is the choice that often must be made. However, most issues, when framed from the perspective of two or more differing points of view, allow for a broader, more reasoned discussion rather than an immediate debate of one view versus an opposite view. If worker security is guaranteed by legislation, for example, it is often thought to be at the expense of the rights of employers, but it might also address what is best in the common interest. With that potential for complexity in mind, then, the following illustrative list of persistent issues and dilemmas is presented:

- individual beliefs/majority rule
- obeying the law/the right to dissent
- cultural variety/cultural assimilation/uniformity
- community progress/individual liberties
- individual rights/public safety

- national security/individual freedom
- national/state/local community control
- worker security/employer rights
- free enterprise/public planning
- global business competition/the national interest

Civic Action

Discussions and arguments about how to deal with these persistent issues and dilemmas go on in families, groups, and the community at large. Social studies should help public discourse to be more enlightened because students possess the knowledge, intellectual skills, and attitudes necessary to confront, discuss, and consider action on such issues. Social studies educators have an obligation to help students explore a variety of positions in a thorough, fair-minded manner. As each position is studied and discussed to determine the strongest points in favor of it, the strongest points in opposition to it, and the consequences that would follow from selecting it, students become better able to improve the ways in which they deal with persistent issues and dilemmas and participate with others in making decisions about them.

Students who possess knowledge, skills, and values are prepared to take appropriate civic action as individuals or as members of groups devoted to civic improvement. Individual and group action designed to support both individual dignity and the common good bring our nation's ideals and practices closer together. In this way, civic participation supports and extends civic ideals and practices in a democratic republic.

How Do We Meet the Social Studies Standards?

No single ingredient can guarantee student achievement of the social studies standards as set forth in this document. In general terms, public commitment, ideal learning conditions, and excellent instruction are equally important and must receive equal attention in educational settings.

Needed: Public Commitment, Time, and Resources

To provide a social studies program of excellence, the ingredient that is most often ignored, yet upon which all others depend, is public commitment. Public commitment requires that the public receive information that clearly demonstrates the importance of social studies programs for the education of all children. Public commitment also requires that the public recognize all that it takes to support excellence in social studies programs.

What does it take? Many things. But when asked to name their most critical need in implementing these standards, teachers, without exception, listed "time." Adequate facilities to foster active learning and house the multitude of materials required to maintain a high-interest laboratory setting are also frequently named by teachers, as are high-quality technology, resources, and opportunities for students to engage in meaningful learning. All of this requires more adequate funding for social studies programs.

Principles of Teaching and Learning

The curriculum standards presented in this document describe major themes and outcome expectations to assure excellence in social studies. The delivery of such a program at the level of classroom teaching is equally important and is discussed at length in the NCSS position statement, "A Vision of Powerful Teaching and Learning in the Social Studies: Building Social Understanding and Civic Efficacy," *Social Education* 57, no. 5 (September 1993): 213–223, reprinted in the back of this volume.

That document identifies and describes those principles of teaching and learning that must undergird all social studies programs of excellence. Those principles are:

1. *Social studies teaching and learning are powerful when they are meaningful.*
   - Students learn connected networks of knowledge, skills, beliefs, and attitudes that they will find useful both in and outside of school.
   - Instruction emphasizes depth of development of important ideas within appropriate breadth of topic coverage and focuses on teaching these important ideas for understanding, appreciation, and life application.
   - The significance and meaningfulness of the content is emphasized both in how it is presented to students and how it is developed through activities.
   - Classroom interaction focuses on sustained examination of a few important topics rather than superficial coverage of many.
   - Meaningful learning activities and assessment strategies focus students' attention on the most important ideas embedded in what they are learning.
   - The teacher is reflective in planning, implementing, and assessing instruction.

2. *Social studies teaching and learning are powerful when they are integrative.*
   - Social studies is integrative in its treatment of topics.
   - It is integrative across time and space.
   - Social studies teaching integrates knowledge, skills, beliefs, values, and attitudes to action.
   - Social studies teaching and learning integrate effective use of technology.
   - Social studies teaching and learning integrate across the curriculum.

3. *Social studies teaching and learning are powerful when they are value-based.*
   - Powerful social studies teaching considers the ethical dimensions of topics and addresses controversial issues, providing an arena for reflective development of concern for the common good and application of social values.
   - Students are made aware of potential social policy implications and taught to think critically and make value-based decisions about related social issues.
   - Rather than promulgating personal, sectarian, or political views, these teachers make sure that students: 1) become aware of the values, complexities, and dilemmas involved in an issue; 2) consider the costs and benefits to various groups that are embedded in potential courses of action; and 3) develop well-reasoned positions consistent with basic democratic social and political values.

- Powerful social studies teaching encourages recognition of opposing points of view, respect for well-supported positions, sensitivity to cultural similarities and differences, and a commitment to social responsibility.

4. *Social studies teaching and learning are powerful when they are challenging.*
- Students are expected to strive to accomplish the instructional goals, both as individuals and as group members.
- Teachers model seriousness of purpose and a thoughtful approach to inquiry and use instructional strategies designed to elicit and support similar qualities from students.
- Teachers show interest in and respect for students' thinking, but demand well-reasoned arguments rather than opinions voiced without adequate thought or commitment.

5. *Social studies teaching and learning are powerful when they are active.*
- Active social studies teaching requires reflective thinking and decision-making as events unfold during instruction.
- Students develop new understanding through a process of active construction of knowledge.
- Interactive discourse facilitates the construction of meaning required to develop important social understanding.
- Teachers gradually move from providing considerable guidance by modeling, explaining, or supplying information that builds student knowledge, to a less directive role that encourages students to become independent and self-regulated learners.
- Powerful social studies teaching emphasizes authentic activities that call for real-life applications using the skills and content of the field.

The teaching and learning document goes on to delineate additional requirements to support an excellent social studies program which lie beyond the control of the individual teacher. These include:
- continuous program assessment;
- preparation of pre-service teachers that is aligned with curriculum and teaching and learning standards;
- provision of in-service training to support teachers in understanding and implementing standards;
- community and governmental support to
  — recognize the subject's vital purpose for civic education
  — sustain teacher education and professional development
  — provide adequate funding and leadership (from school districts and state and federal government).

Introduction

School as a Learning Place

Successful schools are unique places, not simply spaces. When students conceive of a school as space, they focus on "getting through it" as quickly as possible. Time and destination are foremost in their minds. Rather than having learning as the main focus, their objective is to move on, to get through. Society often reinforces this concept of school by using extrinsic motivational clichés like "finish school to earn more money." Extrinsic motivation with its emphasis on time and destination tends to corrupt true learning. Only rarely do we hear, "Stay in school and learn for your sake as a learner."

Our responsibility as educators is to imagine and create places of learning. Such places foster aesthetics, civility, ethics, openness, conversation, security, stewardship/ public responsibility, craftsmanship, and individual liberty. Although all educators must take responsibility for creating a learning place, social studies educators should be leaders in this effort.

Unless this concept of school is taken seriously, with all the necessary resource and time dimensions, curriculum and instruction will remain a symbolic adventure in rhetoric and retribution. Learning is a dependent variable, relying heavily upon a deep sense of place and community within that place. A focus on school as a learning place will help students stop simply moving "through" school and instead find the satisfaction that comes from creating and working within a place that values learning. This focus on school as a place for the community of learners will in the end be advantageous to individuals as well as to society as a whole.

The elements of curriculum; public commitment, time, and resources; powerful teaching and learning; and the concept of school as a learning place are all essential if students are to achieve the social studies standards we advocate.

What Is the Purpose of the Social Studies Standards?

Our world is changing rapidly. Students in our schools today, who will be the citizens of the twenty-first century, are living and learning in the midst of a knowledge explosion unlike any humankind has ever experienced. Because schools and teachers cannot teach everything and because students cannot learn all there is to know, this document focuses on three purposes for these standards. The social studies standards should:

1. serve as a framework for K–12 social studies program design through the use of ten thematic strands;
2. serve as a guide for curriculum decisions by providing performance expectations regarding knowledge, processes, and attitudes essential for all students; and
3. provide examples of classroom practice to guide teachers in designing instruction to help students meet performance expectations.

These social studies standards provide criteria for making decisions as curriculum planners and teachers address such issues as why teach social studies, what to include in the curriculum, how to teach it well to all students, and how to assess whether or not students are able to apply what they have learned. The ten thematic curriculum standards and accompanying sets of student performance expectations constitute an irreducible minimum of what is essential in social studies. Along with the examples of classroom practice, these standards and performance expectations help answer the following questions:

- How can the social studies curriculum help students construct an accurate and positive view of citizenship and become citizens able to address persistent issues, promote civic ideals and practices, and improve our democratic republic?
- What content themes are essential to the curriculum at every level (early, middle, and high school) because they address societal expectations and the needs of young future citizens and are drawn from disciplines and fields related to social studies and from other disciplines and fields that are natural allies of social studies?
- What are the student performance expectations at early, middle, and high school levels for knowledge, skills, attitudes, civic ideals, and practices that encompass social studies as an integrative field?
- How can learning opportunities be structured at each school level to help students meet social studies performance expectations?
- How might performance expectations be assessed to show that students have constructed an understanding that allows them to demonstrate and apply what they have learned?

How Are the Social Studies Standards Organized?

The social studies standards present, in the next chapters of this document, a set of ten thematically based curriculum standards, corresponding sets of performance expectations, and illustrations of exemplary teaching and learning to foster student achievement of the standards at each school level.

A **curriculum standard** is a statement of what should occur programmatically in the formal schooling process; it provides a guiding vision of content and purpose. The social studies curriculum standards, designated by roman numerals, are expressed in thematic statements that begin: "Social studies programs should include experiences that provide for the study of. . . ." These curriculum experiences should enable students to exhibit the knowledge, skills, scholarly perspectives, and commitments to American democratic ideals identified in the **performance expectations**.

For each school level, two or three examples of **classroom activities** related to each theme appear in the "Standards into Practice" chapters (Chapters 4, 5, and 6). In each case, the performance expectations addressed by the example are identified.

Since these themes are interdisciplinary, there is often a close relationship among performance expectations across the curriculum standards. To show these connections, roman numerals representing related themes are cross-referenced in the "Standards into Practice" chapters (Chapters 4, 5, and 6).

Introduction   The ten themes that serve as organizing strands for the social studies curriculum at every school level are:

 I Culture
 II Time, Continuity, and Change
 III People, Places, and Environments
 IV Individual Development and Identity
 V Individuals, Groups, and Institutions
 VI Power, Authority, and Governance
 VII Production, Distribution, and Consumption
 VIII Science, Technology, and Society
 IX Global Connections
 X Civic Ideals and Practices

Two features of these curriculum strands are especially important. First, they are interrelated. To understand culture, for example, students need to understand time, continuity, and change; the relationship among people, places, and environments; and civic ideals and practices. To understand power, authority, and governance, students need to understand the relationship among culture; people, places, and environments; and individuals, groups, and institutions.

Second, the thematic strands draw from all of the social science disciplines and other related disciplines and fields of scholarly study to build a framework for social studies curriculum design. The ten themes thus present a holistic framework for state and local curriculum standards. To further enhance the curriculum design, social studies educators are encouraged to seek detailed content from standards developed for history, geography, civics, economics, and other fields.

Who Can Use the Social Studies Standards and How?

The social studies curriculum standards offer educators, parents, and policymakers the essential conceptual components for curriculum development. Classroom teachers, scholars, and state, district, and school administrators should use this document as a starting point for the systematic development of a K–12 social studies curriculum of excellence.

State governments and departments of education can use the standards to:
- guide change to standards-based education;
- review and evaluate current state curriculum guidelines; and
- develop a state curriculum framework.

School districts and schools can use the standards to:
- provide a framework for curriculum development;
- review and evaluate current social studies programs; and
- provide ideas for instruction and assessment.

Individual teachers can use the standards to:
- provide outcome goals for units and courses;

- evaluate current practices; and
- glean ideas for instruction and assessment.

Parents and community members can use the standards to:
- understand how social studies learning contributes to meeting the broad educational goals of our society;
- assess the quality of social studies education in local school districts; and
- judge children's development as social studies learners.

Teacher educators can use the standards to:
- introduce pre-service and in-service teachers to standards-based planning and curriculum development;
- assess the instructional planning and teaching of pre-service and in-service teachers in their programs and courses; and
- guide the development of pre-service and in-service teacher education programs and courses.

What Is the Relationship of the Social Studies Standards to Other Standards in the Field?

The social studies standards will help teachers, program and curriculum designers, and administrators at the state, district, and school-site levels develop a systematic K–12 social studies program. Using the social studies standards as an umbrella can assist program development by:
- Ensuring integrated, cumulative social studies learning at each level (that is, learning that addresses powerful discipline-based and interdisciplinary themes at the early, middle, and high school levels).
- Encouraging program designers to use the inclusive social studies themes as the basis for a curriculum design that can also draw upon other standards projects (for example, history, geography, civics) for specific grade levels or courses within the K–12 program as appropriate. Most importantly, the several social science disciplines thus find a curriculum "home" in social studies since no one discipline is sufficient in and of itself to meet the vision of social studies as an integrative field.

A metaphor can help readers conceptualize the relationship of social studies and specific, individual disciplines as they promote learning in a K–12 social studies program. Consider a musical ensemble such as an orchestra (the social studies program) as it performs a specific musical composition (a grade level or specific course within the curriculum). At certain times, one instrument (a discipline such as history) takes the lead while others (such as geography and economics) play supporting roles. At other times, several instruments (history, geography, etc.) or the full ensemble play together to fully address the composer's thematic aims. The quality of the performance is the result of the composer's creation of the music (design of the social studies curriculum), the unique qualities of individual instruments (the contribution of individual disciplines), the acoustics of the setting (expertise of curriculum planners and teachers, school site facilities, and instructional resources), and the skills of musicians and the conductor (students, teachers, program planners, and implementers) to know when and how to express the meaning of the composition (curriculum).

There is a rational relationship between the social studies standards and the standards of the several social sciences. The social studies standards address the overall curriculum design and the comprehensive student performance expectations of a program of excellence, while the individual sets of discipline standards provide enhanced content detail to ensure quality instructional programs. Teachers and curriculum designers are encouraged first to establish their program frameworks using the social studies standards as a guide, then to use the individual sets of standards from history, geography, civics, economics, or other disciplines to guide the development of strands and courses within their programs. Using these standards in concert with one another can enable educators to give adequate attention to both integrated and single discipline configurations within the social studies curriculum.

The effective use of the social studies curriculum standards will depend not only on the quality of their design, but also on the skills of educators to know when and how to integrate content, to design quality learning environments, and to construct with these standards more complete K–12 social studies programs that reflect the newest research in learning, developmental abilities of students, and knowledge construction. Only such a thoughtfully designed curriculum will carry forth a vision of social studies for the next century.

Two TEN THEMATIC STRANDS IN SOCIAL STUDIES

This chapter defines and explains the ten thematic strands that form the basis of the social studies standards. The explanations give examples of questions that are asked within each thematic strand, as well as brief overviews of the application of each strand in the early grades, middle grades, and high school.

Ten Strandß ## Culture

Social studies programs should include experiences that provide for the study of culture and cultural diversity.

Human beings create, learn, and adapt culture. Culture helps us to understand ourselves as both individuals and members of various groups. Human cultures exhibit both similarities and differences. We all, for example, have systems of beliefs, knowledge, values, and traditions. Each system also is unique. In a democratic and multicultural society, students need to understand multiple perspectives that derive from different cultural vantage points. This understanding will allow them to relate to people in our nation and throughout the world.

Cultures are dynamic and ever-changing. The study of culture prepares students to ask and answer questions such as: What are the common characteristics of different cultures? How do belief systems, such as religion or political ideals of the culture, influence the other parts of the culture? How does the culture change to accommodate different ideas and beliefs? What does language tell us about the culture? In schools, this theme typically appears in units and courses dealing with geography, history, and anthropology, as well as multicultural topics across the curriculum.

During the early years of school, the exploration of the concepts of likenesses and differences in school subjects such as language arts, mathematics, science, music, and art makes the study of culture appropriate. Socially, the young learner is beginning to interact with other students, some of whom are like the student and some different; naturally, he or she wants to know more about others. In the middle grades, students begin to explore and ask questions about the nature of culture and specific aspects of culture, such as language and beliefs, and the influence of those aspects on human behavior. As students progress through high school, they can understand and use complex cultural concepts such as adaptation, assimilation, acculturation, diffusion, and dissonance drawn from anthropology, sociology, and other disciplines to explain how culture and cultural systems function.

Time, Continuity, & Change

Social studies programs should include experiences that provide for the study of the ways human beings view themselves in and over time.

Human beings seek to understand their historical roots and to locate themselves in time. Such understanding involves knowing what things were like in the past and how things change and develop. Knowing how to read and reconstruct the past allows one to develop a historical perspective and to answer questions such as: Who am I? What happened in the past? How am I connected to those in the past? How has the world changed and how might it change in the future? Why does our personal sense of relatedness to the past change? How can the perspective we have about our own life experiences be viewed as part of the larger human story across time? How do our personal stories reflect varying points of view and inform contemporary ideas and actions?

This theme typically appears in courses that: 1) include perspectives from various aspects of history; 2) draw upon historical knowledge during the examination of social issues; and 3) develop the habits of mind that historians and scholars in the humanities and social sciences employ to study the past and its relationship to the present in the United States and other societies.

Learners in early grades gain experience with sequencing to establish a sense of order and time. They enjoy hearing stories of the recent past as well as of long ago. In addition, they begin to recognize that individuals may hold different views about the past and to understand the linkages between human decisions and consequences. Thus, the foundation is laid for the development of historical knowledge, skills, and values. In the middle grades, students, through a more formal study of history, continue to expand their understanding of the past and of historical concepts and inquiry. They begin to understand and appreciate differences in historical perspectives, recognizing that interpretations are influenced by individual experiences, societal values, and cultural traditions. High school students engage in more sophisticated analysis and reconstruction of the past, examining its relationship to the present and extrapolating into the future. They integrate individual stories about people, events, and situations to form a more holistic conception, in which continuity and change are linked in time and across cultures. Students also learn to draw on their knowledge of history to make informed choices and decisions in the present.

Ten Strands

People, Places, & Environments

Social studies programs should include experiences that provide for the study of people, places, and environments.

Technological advances connect students at all levels to the world beyond their personal locations. The study of people, places, and human-environment interactions assists learners as they create their spatial views and geographic perspectives of the world. Today's social, cultural, economic, and civic demands on individuals mean that students will need the knowledge, skills, and understanding to ask and answer questions such as: Where are things located? Why are they located where they are? What patterns are reflected in the groupings of things? What do we mean by region? How do landforms change? What implications do these changes have for people? This area of study helps learners make informed and critical decisions about the relationship between human beings and their environment. In schools, this theme typically appears in units and courses dealing with area studies and geography.

In the early grades, young learners draw upon immediate personal experiences as a basis for exploring geographic concepts and skills. They also express interest in things distant and unfamiliar and have concern for the use and abuse of the physical environment. During the middle school years, students relate their personal experiences to happenings in other environmental contexts. Appropriate experiences will encourage increasingly abstract thought as students use data and apply skills in analyzing human behavior in relation to its physical and cultural environment. Students in high school are able to apply geographic understanding across a broad range of fields, including the fine arts, sciences, and humanities. Geographic concepts become central to learners' comprehension of global connections as they expand their knowledge of diverse cultures, both historical and contemporary. The importance of core geographic themes to public policy is recognized and should be explored as students address issues of domestic and international significance.

Individual Development & Identity

Social studies programs should include experiences that provide for the study of individual development and identity.

Personal identity is shaped by one's culture, by groups, and by institutional influences. How do people learn? Why do people behave as they do? What influences how people learn, perceive, and grow? How do people meet their basic needs in a variety of contexts? Questions such as these are central to the study of how individuals develop from youth to adulthood. Examination of various forms of human behavior enhances understanding of the relationships among social norms and emerging personal identities, the social processes that influence identity formation, and the ethical principles underlying individual action. In schools, this theme typically appears in units and courses dealing with psychology and anthropology.

Given the nature of individual development and our own cultural context, students need to be aware of the processes of learning, growth, and development at every level of their school experience. In the early grades, for example, observing brothers, sisters, and older adults, looking at family photo albums, remembering past achievements and projecting oneself into the future, and comparing the patterns of behavior evident in people of different age groups are appropriate activities because young learners develop their personal identities in the context of families, peers, schools, and communities. Central to this development are the exploration, identification, and analysis of how individuals relate to others. In the middle grades, issues of personal identity are refocused as the individual begins to explain self in relation to others in the society and culture. At the high school level, students need to encounter multiple opportunities to examine contemporary patterns of human behavior, using methods from the behavioral sciences to apply core concepts drawn from psychology, social psychology, sociology, and anthropology as they apply to individuals, societies, and cultures.

Ten Strands ## Individuals, Groups, & Institutions

Social studies programs should include experiences that provide for the study of interactions among individuals, groups, and institutions.

Institutions such as schools, churches, families, government agencies, and the courts all play an integral role in our lives. These and other institutions exert enormous influence over us, yet institutions are no more than organizational embodiments to further the core social values of those who comprise them. Thus, it is important that students know how institutions are formed, what controls and influences them, how they control and influence individuals and culture, and how institutions can be maintained or changed. The study of individuals, groups, and institutions, drawing upon sociology, anthropology, and other disciplines, prepares students to ask and answer questions such as: What is the role of institutions in this and other societies? How am I influenced by institutions? How do institutions change? What is my role in institutional change? In schools, this theme typically appears in units and courses dealing with sociology, anthropology, psychology, political science, and history.

Young children should be given opportunities to examine various institutions that affect their lives and influence their thinking. They should be assisted in recognizing the tensions that occur when the goals, values, and principles of two or more institutions or groups conflict—for example, when the school board prohibits candy machines in schools vs. a class project to install a candy machine to help raise money for the local hospital. They should also have opportunities to explore ways in which institutions such as churches or health care networks are created to respond to changing individual and group needs. Middle school learners will benefit from varied experiences through which they examine the ways in which institutions change over time, promote social conformity, and influence culture. They should be encouraged to use this understanding to suggest ways to work through institutional change for the common good. High school students must understand the paradigms and traditions that undergird social and political institutions. They should be provided opportunities to examine, use, and add to the body of knowledge related to the behavioral sciences and social theory as it relates to the ways people and groups organize themselves around common needs, beliefs, and interests.

Power, Authority, & Governance

Social studies programs should include experiences that provide for the study of how people create and change structures of power, authority, and governance.

Understanding the historical development of structures of power, authority, and governance and their evolving functions in contemporary U.S. society, as well as in other parts of the world, is essential for developing civic competence. In exploring this theme, students confront questions such as: What is power? What forms does it take? Who holds it? How is it gained, used, and justified? What is legitimate authority? How are governments created, structured, maintained, and changed? How can we keep government responsive to its citizens' needs and interests? How can individual rights be protected within the context of majority rule? By examining the purposes and characteristics of various governance systems, learners develop an understanding of how groups and nations attempt to resolve conflicts and seek to establish order and security. Through study of the dynamic relationships among individual rights and responsibilities, the needs of social groups, and concepts of a just society, learners become more effective problem-solvers and decision-makers when addressing the persistent issues and social problems encountered in public life. They do so by applying concepts and methods of political science and law. In schools, this theme typically appears in units and courses dealing with government, politics, political science, history, law, and other social sciences.

Learners in the early grades explore their natural and developing sense of fairness and order as they experience relationships with others. They develop an increasingly comprehensive awareness of rights and responsibilities in specific contexts. During the middle school years, these rights and responsibilities are applied in more complex contexts with emphasis on new applications. High school students develop their abilities in the use of abstract principles. They study the various systems that have been developed over the centuries to allocate and employ power and authority in the governing process. At every level, learners should have opportunities to apply their knowledge and skills to and participate in the workings of the various levels of power, authority, and governance.

Ten Strands

Production, Distribution, & Consumption

Social studies programs should include experiences that provide for the study of how people organize for the production, distribution, and consumption of goods and services.

People have wants that often exceed the limited resources available to them. As a result, a variety of ways have been invented to decide upon answers to four fundamental questions: What is to be produced? How is production to be organized? How are goods and services to be distributed? What is the most effective allocation of the factors of production (land, labor, capital, and management)? Unequal distribution of resources necessitates systems of exchange, including trade, to improve the well-being of the economy, while the role of government in economic policymaking varies over time and from place to place. Increasingly these decisions are global in scope and require systematic study of an interdependent world economy and the role of technology in economic decision-making. In schools, this theme typically appears in units and courses dealing with concepts, principles, and issues drawn from the discipline of economics.

Young learners begin by differentiating between wants and needs. They explore economic decisions as they compare their own economic experiences with those of others and consider the wider consequences of those decisions on groups, communities, the nation, and beyond. In the middle grades, learners expand their knowledge of economic concepts and principles, and use economic reasoning processes in addressing issues related to the four fundamental economic questions. High school students develop economic perspectives and deeper understanding of key economic concepts and processes through systematic study of a range of economic and sociopolitical systems, with particular emphasis on the examination of domestic and global economic policy options related to matters such as health care, resource use, unemployment, and trade.

Science, Technology, & Society

Social studies programs should include experiences that provide for the study of relationships among science, technology, and society.

Technology is as old as the first crude tool invented by prehistoric humans, but today's technology forms the basis for some of our most difficult social choices. Modern life as we know it would be impossible without technology and the science that supports it. But technology brings with it many questions: Is new technology always better than that which it will replace? What can we learn from the past about how new technologies result in broader social change, some of which is unanticipated? How can we cope with the ever-increasing pace of change, perhaps even with the feeling that technology has gotten out of control? How can we manage technology so that the greatest number of people benefit from it? How can we preserve our fundamental values and beliefs in a world that is rapidly becoming one technology-linked village? This theme appears in units or courses dealing with history, geography, economics, and civics and government. It draws upon several scholarly fields from the natural and physical sciences, social sciences, and the humanities for specific examples of issues and the knowledge base for considering responses to the societal issues related to science and technology.

Young children can learn how technologies form systems and how their daily lives are intertwined with a host of technologies. They can study how basic technologies such as ships, automobiles, and airplanes have evolved and how we have employed technology such as air conditioning, dams, and irrigation to modify our physical environment. From history (their own and others'), they can construct examples of how technologies such as the wheel, the stirrup, and the transistor radio altered the course of history. By the middle grades, students can begin to explore the complex relationships among technology, human values, and behavior. They will find that science and technology bring changes that surprise us and even challenge our beliefs, as in the case of discoveries and their applications related to our universe, the genetic basis of life, atomic physics, and others. As they move from the middle grades to high school, students will need to think more deeply about how we can manage technology so that we control it rather than the other way around. There should be opportunities to confront such issues as the consequences of using robots to produce goods, the protection of privacy in the age of computers and electronic surveillance, and the opportunities and challenges of genetic engineering, test-tube life, and medical technology with all their implications for longevity and quality of life and religious beliefs.

Ten Strands ## Global Connections

Social studies programs should include experiences that provide for the study of global connections and interdependence.

The realities of global interdependence require understanding the increasingly important and diverse global connections among world societies. Analysis of tensions between national interests and global priorities contributes to the development of possible solutions to persistent and emerging global issues in many fields: health care, economic development, environmental quality, universal human rights, and others. Analyzing patterns and relationships within and among world cultures, such as economic competition and interdependence, age-old ethnic enmities, political and military alliances, and others, helps learners carefully examine policy alternatives that have both national and global implications. This theme typically appears in units or courses dealing with geography, culture, and economics, but again can draw upon the natural and physical sciences and the humanities, including literature, the arts, and language.

Through exposure to various media and first-hand experiences, young learners become aware of and are affected by events on a global scale. Within this context, students in early grades examine and explore global connections and basic issues and concerns, suggesting and initiating responsive action plans. In the middle years, learners can initiate analysis of the interactions among states and nations and their cultural complexities as they respond to global events and changes. At the high school level, students are able to think systematically about personal, national, and global decisions, interactions, and consequences, including addressing critical issues such as peace, human rights, trade, and global ecology.

Civic Ideals & Practices

Social studies programs should include experiences that provide for the study of the ideals, principles, and practices of citizenship in a democratic republic.

An understanding of civic ideals and practices of citizenship is critical to full participation in society and is a central purpose of the social studies. All people have a stake in examining civic ideals and practices across time and in diverse societies as well as at home, and in determining how to close the gap between present practices and the ideals upon which our democratic republic is based. Learners confront such questions as: What is civic participation and how can I be involved? How has the meaning of citizenship evolved? What is the balance between rights and responsibilities? What is the role of the citizen in the community and the nation, and as a member of the world community? How can I make a positive difference? In schools, this theme typically appears in units or courses dealing with history, political science, cultural anthropology, and fields such as global studies and law-related education, while also drawing upon content from the humanities.

In the early grades, students are introduced to civic ideals and practices through activities such as helping to set classroom expectations, examining experiences in relation to ideals, and determining how to balance the needs of individuals and the group. During these years, children also experience views of citizenship in other times and places through stories and drama. By the middle grades, students expand their ability to analyze and evaluate the relationships between ideals and practice. They are able to see themselves taking civic roles in their communities. High school students increasingly recognize the rights and responsibilities of citizens in identifying societal needs, setting directions for public policies, and working to support both individual dignity and the common good. They learn by experience how to participate in community service and political activities and how to use democratic process to influence public policy.

Three **STANDARDS AND PERFORMANCE EXPECTATIONS FOR EARLY GRADES, MIDDLE GRADES, AND HIGH SCHOOL: REFERENCE CHARTS**

Performance
Expectations

 *Culture*

Social studies programs should include experiences that provide for the study of *culture and cultural diversity,* so that the learner can:

Early Grades	Middle Grades	High School
a. explore and describe similarities and differences in the ways groups, societies, and cultures address similar human needs and concerns;	a. compare similarities and differences in the ways groups, societies, and cultures meet human needs and concerns;	a. analyze and explain the ways groups, societies, and cultures address human needs and concerns;
b. give examples of how experiences may be interpreted differently by people from diverse cultural perspectives and frames of reference;	b. explain how information and experiences may be interpreted by people from diverse cultural perspectives and frames of reference;	b. predict how data and experiences may be interpreted by people from diverse cultural perspectives and frames of reference;
c. describe ways in which language, stories, folktales, music, and artistic creations serve as expressions of culture and influence behavior of people living in a particular culture;	c. explain and give examples of how language, literature, the arts, architecture, other artifacts, traditions, beliefs, values, and behaviors contribute to the development and transmission of culture;	c. apply an understanding of culture as an integrated whole that explains the functions and interactions of language, literature, the arts, traditions, beliefs and values, and behavior patterns;
d. compare ways in which people from different cultures think about and deal with their physical environment and social conditions;	d. explain why individuals and groups respond differently to their physical and social environments and/or changes to them on the basis of shared assumptions, values, and beliefs;	d. compare and analyze societal patterns for preserving and transmitting culture while adapting to environmental or social change;
e. give examples and describe the importance of cultural unity and diversity within and across groups.	e. articulate the implications of cultural diversity, as well as cohesion, within and across groups.	e. demonstrate the value of cultural diversity, as well as cohesion, within and across groups;
		f. interpret patterns of behavior reflecting values and attitudes that contribute or pose obstacles to cross-cultural understanding;
		g. construct reasoned judgments about specific cultural responses to persistent human issues;
		h. explain and apply ideas, theories, and modes of inquiry drawn from anthropology and sociology in the examination of persistent issues and social problems.

❶ *Time, Continuity, & Change*

Social studies programs should include experiences that provide for the study of *the ways human beings view themselves in and over time*, so that the learner can:

Early Grades	Middle Grades	High School
a. demonstrate an understanding that different people may describe the same event or situation in diverse ways, citing reasons for the differences in views;	a. demonstrate an understanding that different scholars may describe the same event or situation in different ways but must provide reasons or evidence for their views;	a. demonstrate that historical knowledge and the concept of time are socially influenced constructions that lead historians to be selective in the questions they seek to answer and the evidence they use;
b. demonstrate an ability to use correctly vocabulary associated with time such as past, present, future, and long ago; read and construct simple timelines; identify examples of change; and recognize examples of cause and effect relationships;	b. identify and use key concepts such as chronology, causality, change, conflict, and complexity to explain, analyze, and show connections among patterns of historical change and continuity;	b. apply key concepts such as time, chronology, causality, change, conflict, and complexity to explain, analyze, and show connections among patterns of historical change and continuity;
c. compare and contrast different stories or accounts about past events, people, places, or situations, identifying how they contribute to our understanding of the past;	c. identify and describe selected historical periods and patterns of change within and across cultures, such as the rise of civilizations, the development of transportation systems, the growth and breakdown of colonial systems, and others;	c. identify and describe significant historical periods and patterns of change within and across cultures, such as the development of ancient cultures and civilizations, the rise of nation-states, and social, economic, and political revolutions;
d. identify and use various sources for reconstructing the past, such as documents, letters, diaries, maps, textbooks, photos, and others;	d. identify and use processes important to reconstructing and reinterpreting the past, such as using a variety of sources, providing, validating, and weighing evidence for claims, checking credibility of sources, and searching for causality;	d. systematically employ processes of critical historical inquiry to reconstruct and reinterpret the past, such as using a variety of sources and checking their credibility, validating and weighing evidence for claims, and searching for causality;
e. demonstrate an understanding that people in different times and places view the world differently;	e. develop critical sensitivities such as empathy and skepticism regarding attitudes, values, and behaviors of people in different historical contexts;	e. investigate, interpret, and analyze multiple historical and contemporary viewpoints within and across cultures related to important events, recurring dilemmas, and persistent issues, while employing empathy, skepticism, and critical judgement;
f. use knowledge of facts and concepts drawn from history, along with elements of historical inquiry, to inform decision-making about and action-taking on public issues.	f. use knowledge of facts and concepts drawn from history, along with methods of historical inquiry, to inform decision-making about and action-taking on public issues.	f. apply ideas, theories, and modes of historical inquiry to analyze historical and contemporary developments, and to inform and evaluate actions concerning public policy issues.

Performance Expectations

III *People, Places, & Environments*

Social studies programs should include experiences that provide for the study of *people, places, and environments*, so that the learner can:

Early Grades	Middle Grades	High School
a. construct and use mental maps of locales, regions, and the world that demonstrate understanding of relative location, direction, size, and shape;	a. elaborate mental maps of locales, regions, and the world that demonstrate understanding of relative location, direction, size, and shape;	a. refine mental maps of locales, regions, and the world that demonstrate understanding of relative location, direction, size, and shape;
b. interpret, use, and distinguish various representations of the earth, such as maps, globes, and photographs;	b. create, interpret, use, and distinguish various representations of the earth, such as maps, globes, and photographs;	b. create, interpret, use, and synthesize information from various representations of the earth, such as maps, globes, and photographs;
c. use appropriate resources, data sources, and geographic tools such as atlases, data bases, grid systems, charts, graphs, and maps to generate, manipulate, and interpret information;	c. use appropriate resources, data sources, and geographic tools such as aerial photographs, satellite images, geographic information systems (GIS), map projections, and cartography to generate, manipulate, and interpret information such as atlases, data bases, grid systems, charts, graphs, and maps;	c. use appropriate resources, data sources, and geographic tools such as aerial photographs, satellite images, geographic information systems (GIS), map projections, and cartography to generate, manipulate, and interpret information such as atlases, data bases, grid systems, charts, graphs, and maps;
d. estimate distance and calculate scale;	d. estimate distance, calculate scale, and distinguish other geographic relationships such as population density and spatial distribution patterns;	d. calculate distance, scale, area, and density, and distinguish spatial distribution patterns;
e. locate and distinguish among varying landforms and geographic features, such as mountains, plateaus, islands, and oceans;	e. locate and describe varying landforms and geographic features, such as mountains, plateaus, islands, rain forests, deserts, and oceans, and explain their relationships within the ecosystem;	e. describe, differentiate, and explain the relationships among various regional and global patterns of geographic phenomena such as landforms, soils, climate, vegetation, natural resources, and population;
f. describe and speculate about physical system changes, such as seasons, climate and weather, and the water cycle;	f. describe physical system changes such as seasons, climate and weather, and the water cycle and identify geographic patterns associated with them;	f. use knowledge of physical system changes such as seasons, climate and weather, and the water cycle to explain geographic phenomena;
g. describe how people create places that reflect ideas, personality, culture, and wants and needs as they design homes, playgrounds, classrooms, and the like;	g. describe how people create places that reflect cultural values and ideals as they build neighborhoods, parks, shopping centers, and the like;	g. describe and compare how people create places that reflect culture, human needs, government policy, and current values and ideals as they design and build specialized buildings, neighborhoods, shopping centers, urban centers, industrial parks, and the like;

Early Grades	Middle Grades	High School
h. examine the interaction of human beings and their physical environment, the use of land, building of cities, and ecosystem changes in selected locales and regions;	h. examine, interpret, and analyze physical and cultural patterns and their interactions, such as land use, settlement patterns, cultural transmission of customs and ideas, and ecosystem changes;	h. examine, interpret, and analyze physical and cultural patterns and their interactions, such as land use, settlement patterns, cultural transmission of customs and ideas, and ecosystem changes;
i. explore ways that the earth's physical features have changed over time in the local region and beyond and how these changes may be connected to one another;	i. describe ways that historical events have been influenced by, and have influenced, physical and human geographic factors in local, regional, national, and global settings;	i. describe and assess ways that historical events have been influenced by, and have influenced, physical and human geographic factors in local, regional, national, and global settings;
j. observe and speculate about social and economic effects of environmental changes and crises resulting from phenomena such as floods, storms, and drought;	j. observe and speculate about social and economic effects of environmental changes and crises resulting from phenomena such as floods, storms, and drought;	j. analyze and evaluate social and economic effects of environmental changes and crises resulting from phenomena such as floods, storms, and drought;
k. consider existing uses and propose and evaluate alternative uses of resources and land in home, school, community, the region, and beyond.	k. propose, compare, and evaluate alternative uses of land and resources in communities, regions, nations, and the world.	k. propose, compare, and evaluate alternative policies for the use of land and other resources in communities, regions, nations, and the world.

ⅣV *Individual Development & Identity*

Social studies programs should include experiences that provide for the study of *individual development and identity*, so that the learner can:

Early Grades	Middle Grades	High School
a. describe personal changes over time, such as those related to physical development and personal interests;	a. relate personal changes to social, cultural, and historical contexts;	a. articulate personal connections to time, place, and social/cultural systems;
b. describe personal connections to place—especially place as associated with immediate surroundings;	b. describe personal connections to place—as associated with community, nation, and world;	b. identify, describe, and express appreciation for the influences of various historical and contemporary cultures on an individual's daily life;
c. describe the unique features of one's nuclear and extended families;	c. describe the ways family, gender, ethnicity, nationality, and institutional affiliations contribute to personal identity;	c. describe the ways family, religion, gender, ethnicity, nationality, socioeconomic status, and other group and cultural influences contribute to the development of a sense of self;
d. show how learning and physical development affect behavior;	d. relate such factors as physical endowment and capabilities, learning, motivation, personality, perception, and behavior to individual development;	d. apply concepts, methods, and theories about the study of human growth and development, such as physical endowment, learning, motivation, behavior, perception, and personality;
e. identify and describe ways family, groups, and community influence the individual's daily life and personal choices;	e. identify and describe ways regional, ethnic, and national cultures influence individuals' daily lives;	e. examine the interactions of ethnic, national, or cultural influences in specific situations or events;
f. explore factors that contribute to one's personal identity such as interests, capabilities, and perceptions;	f. identify and describe the influence of perception, attitudes, values, and beliefs on personal identity;	f. analyze the role of perceptions, attitudes, values, and beliefs in the development of personal identity;
g. analyze a particular event to identify reasons individuals might respond to it in different ways;	g. identify and interpret examples of stereotyping, conformity, and altruism;	g. compare and evaluate the impact of stereotyping, conformity, acts of altruism, and other behaviors on individuals and groups;
h. work independently and cooperatively to accomplish goals.	h. work independently and cooperatively to accomplish goals.	h. work independently and cooperatively within groups and institutions to accomplish goals;
		i. examine factors that contribute to and damage one's mental health and analyze issues related to mental health and behavioral disorders in contemporary society.

Ⓥ Individuals, Groups, & Institutions

Social studies programs should include experiences that provide for the study of *interactions among individuals, groups, and institutions*, so that the learner can:

Early Grades	Middle Grades	High School
a. identify roles as learned behavior patterns in group situations such as student, family member, peer play group member, or club member;	a. demonstrate an understanding of concepts such as role, status, and social class in describing the interactions of individuals and social groups;	a. apply concepts such as role, status, and social class in describing the connections and interactions of individuals, groups, and institutions in society;
b. give examples of and explain group and institutional influences such as religious beliefs, laws, and peer pressure, on people, events, and elements of culture;	b. analyze group and institutional influences on people, events, and elements of culture;	b. analyze group and institutional influences on people, events, and elements of culture in both historical and contemporary settings;
c. identify examples of institutions and describe the interactions of people with institutions;	c. describe the various forms institutions take and the interactions of people with institutions;	c. describe the various forms institutions take, and explain how they develop and change over time;
d. identify and describe examples of tensions between and among individuals, groups, or institutions, and how belonging to more than one group can cause internal conflicts;	d. identify and analyze examples of tensions between expressions of individuality and group or institutional efforts to promote social conformity;	d. identify and analyze examples of tensions between expressions of individuality and efforts used to promote social conformity by groups and institutions;
e. identify and describe examples of tension between an individual's beliefs and government policies and laws;	e. identify and describe examples of tensions between belief systems and government policies and laws;	e. describe and examine belief systems basic to specific traditions and laws in contemporary and historical movements;
f. give examples of the role of institutions in furthering both continuity and change;	f. describe the role of institutions in furthering both continuity and change;	f. evaluate the role of institutions in furthering both continuity and change;
g. show how groups and institutions work to meet individual needs and promote the common good, and identify examples of where they fail to do so.	g. apply knowledge of how groups and institutions work to meet individual needs and promote the common good.	g. analyze the extent to which groups and institutions meet individual needs and promote the common good in contemporary and historical settings;
		h. explain and apply ideas and modes of inquiry drawn from behavioral science and social theory in the examination of persistent issues and social problems.

Ⅵ *Power, Authority, & Governance*

Social studies programs should include experiences that provide for the study of *how people create and change structures of power, authority, and governance,* so that the learner can:

Early Grades	Middle Grades	High School
a. examine the rights and responsibilities of the individual in relation to his or her social group, such as family, peer group, and school class;	a. examine persistent issues involving the rights, roles, and status of the individual in relation to the general welfare;	a. examine persistent issues involving the rights, roles, and status of the individual in relation to the general welfare;
b. explain the purpose of government;	b. describe the purpose of government and how its powers are acquired, used, and justified;	b. explain the purpose of government and analyze how its powers are acquired, used, and justified;
c. give examples of how government does or does not provide for needs and wants of people, establish order and security, and manage conflict;	c. analyze and explain ideas and governmental mechanisms to meet needs and wants of citizens, regulate territory, manage conflict, and establish order and security;	c. analyze and explain ideas and mechanisms to meet needs and wants of citizens, regulate territory, manage conflict, establish order and security, and balance competing conceptions of a just society;
d. recognize how groups and organizations encourage unity and deal with diversity to maintain order and security;	d. describe the ways nations and organizations respond to forces of unity and diversity affecting order and security;	d. compare and analyze the ways nations and organizations respond to conflicts between forces of unity and forces of diversity;
e. distinguish among local, state, and national government and identify representative leaders at these levels such as mayor, governor, and president;	e. identify and describe the basic features of the political system in the United States, and identify representative leaders from various levels and branches of government;	e. compare different political systems (their ideologies, structure, institutions, processes, and political cultures) with that of the United States, and identify representative political leaders from selected historical and contemporary settings;
f. identify and describe factors that contribute to cooperation and cause disputes within and among groups and nations;	f. explain conditions, actions, and motivations that contribute to conflict and cooperation within and among nations;	f. analyze and evaluate conditions, actions, and motivations that contribute to conflict and cooperation within and among nations;
g. explore the role of technology in communications, transportation, information-processing, weapons development, or other areas as it contributes to or helps resolve conflicts;	g. describe and analyze the role of technology in communications, transportation, information-processing, weapons development, or other areas as it contributes to or helps resolve conflicts;	g. evaluate the role of technology in communications, transportation, information-processing, weapons development, or other areas as it contributes to or helps resolve conflicts;
h. recognize and give examples of the tensions between the wants and needs of individuals and groups, and concepts such as fairness, equity, and justice.	h. explain and apply concepts such as power, role, status, justice, and influence to the examination of persistent issues and social problems;	h. explain and apply ideas, theories, and modes of inquiry drawn from political science to the examination of persistent issues and social problems;

Early Grades	Middle Grades	High School
	i. give examples and explain how governments attempt to achieve their stated ideals at home and abroad.	i. evaluate the extent to which governments achieve their stated ideals and policies at home and abroad; j. prepare a public policy paper and present and defend it before an appropriate forum in school or community.

⑦ *Production, Distribution, & Consumption*

Social studies programs should include experiences that provide for the study of *how people organize for the production, distribution, and consumption of goods and services,* so that the learner can:

Early Grades	Middle Grades	High School
a. give examples that show how scarcity and choice govern our economic decisions;	a. give and explain examples of ways that economic systems structure choices about how goods and services are to be produced and distributed;	a. explain how the scarcity of productive resources (human, capital, technological, and natural) requires the development of economic systems to make decisions about how goods and services are to be produced and distributed;
b. distinguish between needs and wants;	b. describe the role that supply and demand, prices, incentives, and profits play in determining what is produced and distributed in a competitive market system;	b. analyze the role that supply and demand, prices, incentives, and profits play in determining what is produced and distributed in a competitive market system;
c. identify examples of private and public goods and services;	c. explain the difference between private and public goods and services;	c. consider the costs and benefits to society of allocating goods and services through private and public sectors;
d. give examples of the various institutions that make up economic systems such as families, workers, banks, labor unions, government agencies, small businesses, and large corporations;	d. describe a range of examples of the various institutions that make up economic systems such as households, business firms, banks, government agencies, labor unions, and corporations;	d. describe relationships among the various economic institutions that comprise economic systems such as households, business firms, banks, government agencies, labor unions, and corporations;
e. describe how we depend upon workers with specialized jobs and the ways in which they contribute to the production and exchange of goods and services;	e. describe the role of specialization and exchange in the economic process;	e. analyze the role of specialization and exchange in economic processes;
f. describe the influence of incentives, values, traditions, and habits on economic decisions;	f. explain and illustrate how values and beliefs influence different economic decisions;	f. compare how values and beliefs influence economic decisions in different societies;
g. explain and demonstrate the role of money in everyday life;	g. differentiate among various forms of exchange and money;	g. compare basic economic systems according to how rules and procedures deal with demand, supply, prices, the role of government, banks, labor and labor unions, savings and investments, and capital;
h. describe the relationship of price to supply and demand;	h. compare basic economic systems according to who determines what is produced, distributed, and consumed;	h. apply economic concepts and reasoning when evaluating historical and contemporary social developments and issues;

Early Grades	**Middle Grades**	**High School**
i. use economic concepts such as supply, demand, and price to help explain events in the community and nation;	i. use economic concepts to help explain historical and current developments and issues in local, national, or global contexts;	i. distinguish between the domestic and global economic systems, and explain how the two interact;
j. apply knowledge of economic concepts in developing a response to a current local economic issue, such as how to reduce the flow of trash into a rapidly filling landfill.	j. use economic reasoning to compare different proposals for dealing with a contemporary social issue such as unemployment, acid rain, or high quality education.	j. apply knowledge of production, distribution, and consumption in the analysis of a public issue such as the allocation of health care or the consumption of energy, and devise an economic plan for accomplishing a socially desirable outcome related to that issue;
		k. distinguish between economics as a field of inquiry and the economy.

⒅ *Science, Technology, & Society*

Social studies programs should include experiences that provide for the study of *relationships among science, technology, and society,* so that the learner can:

Early Grades	Middle Grades	High School
a. identify and describe examples in which science and technology have changed the lives of people, such as in homemaking, childcare, work, transportation, and communication;	a. examine and describe the influence of culture on scientific and technological choices and advancement, such as in transportation, medicine, and warfare;	a. identify and describe both current and historical examples of the interaction and interdependence of science, technology, and society in a variety of cultural settings;
b. identify and describe examples in which science and technology have led to changes in the physical environment, such as the building of dams and levees, offshore oil drilling, medicine from rain forests, and loss of rain forests due to extraction of resources or alternative uses;	b. show through specific examples how science and technology have changed people's perceptions of the social and natural world, such as in their relationship to the land, animal life, family life, and economic needs, wants, and security;	b. make judgments about how science and technology have transformed the physical world and human society and our understanding of time, space, place, and human-environment interactions;
c. describe instances in which changes in values, beliefs, and attitudes have resulted from new scientific and technological knowledge, such as conservation of resources and awareness of chemicals harmful to life and the environment;	c. describe examples in which values, beliefs, and attitudes have been influenced by new scientific and technological knowledge, such as the invention of the printing press, conceptions of the universe, applications of atomic energy, and genetic discoveries;	c. analyze how science and technology influence the core values, beliefs, and attitudes of society, and how core values, beliefs, and attitudes of society shape scientific and technological change;
d. identify examples of laws and policies that govern scientific and technological applications, such as the Endangered Species Act and environmental protection policies;	d. explain the need for laws and policies to govern scientific and technological applications, such as in the safety and well-being of workers and consumers and the regulation of utilities, radio, and television;	d. evaluate various policies that have been proposed as ways of dealing with social changes resulting from new technologies, such as genetically engineered plants and animals;
e. suggest ways to monitor science and technology in order to protect the physical environment, individual rights, and the common good.	e. seek reasonable and ethical solutions to problems that arise when scientific advancements and social norms or values come into conflict.	e. recognize and interpret varied perspectives about human societies and the physical world using scientific knowledge, ethical standards, and technologies from diverse world cultures;
		f. formulate strategies and develop policies for influencing public discussions associated with technology-society issues, such as the greenhouse effect.

Ⓘ Global Connections

Social studies programs should include experiences that provide for the study of *global connections and interdependence*, so that the learner can:

Early Grades	Middle Grades	High School
a. explore ways that language, art, music, belief systems, and other cultural elements may facilitate global understanding or lead to misunderstanding;	a. describe instances in which language, art, music, belief systems, and other cultural elements can facilitate global understanding or cause misunderstanding;	a. explain how language, art, music, belief systems, and other cultural elements can facilitate global understanding or cause misunderstanding;
b. give examples of conflict, cooperation, and interdependence among individuals, groups, and nations;	b. analyze examples of conflict, cooperation, and interdependence among groups, societies, and nations;	b. explain conditions and motivations that contribute to conflict, cooperation, and interdependence among groups, societies, and nations;
c. examine the effects of changing technologies on the global community;	c. describe and analyze the effects of changing technologies on the global community;	c. analyze and evaluate the effects of changing technologies on the global community;
d. explore causes, consequences, and possible solutions to persistent, contemporary, and emerging global issues, such as pollution and endangered species;	d. explore the causes, consequences, and possible solutions to persistent, contemporary, and emerging global issues, such as health, security, resource allocation, economic development, and environmental quality;	d. analyze the causes, consequences, and possible solutions to persistent, contemporary, and emerging global issues, such as health, security, resource allocation, economic development, and environmental quality;
e. examine the relationships and tensions between personal wants and needs and various global concerns, such as use of imported oil, land use, and environmental protection;	e. describe and explain the relationships and tensions between national sovereignty and global interests, in such matters as territory, natural resources, trade, use of technology, and welfare of people;	e. analyze the relationships and tensions between national sovereignty and global interests, in such matters as territory, economic development, nuclear and other weapons, use of natural resources, and human rights concerns;
f. investigate concerns, issues, standards, and conflicts related to universal human rights, such as the treatment of children, religious groups, and effects of war.	f. demonstrate understanding of concerns, standards, issues, and conflicts related to universal human rights;	f. analyze or formulate policy statements demonstrating an understanding of concerns, standards, issues, and conflicts related to universal human rights;
	g. identify and describe the roles of international and multinational organizations.	g. describe and evaluate the role of international and multinational organizations in the global arena;
		h. illustrate how individual behaviors and decisions connect with global systems.

ⓧ *Civic Ideals & Practices*

Social studies programs should include experiences that provide for the study of *the ideals, principles, and practices of citizenship in a democratic republic,* so that the learner can:

Early Grades	Middle Grades	High School
a. identify key ideals of the United States' democratic republican form of government, such as individual human dignity, liberty, justice, equality, and the rule of law, and discuss their application in specific situations;	a. examine the origins and continuing influence of key ideals of the democratic republican form of government, such as individual human dignity, liberty, justice, equality, and the rule of law;	a. explain the origins and interpret the continuing influence of key ideals of the democratic republican form of government, such as individual human dignity, liberty, justice, equality, and the rule of law;
b. identify examples of rights and responsibilities of citizens;	b. identify and interpret sources and examples of the rights and responsibilities of citizens;	b. identify, analyze, interpret, and evaluate sources and examples of citizens' rights and responsibilities;
c. locate, access, organize, and apply information about an issue of public concern from multiple points of view;	c. locate, access, analyze, organize, and apply information about selected public issues—recognizing and explaining multiple points of view;	c. locate, access, analyze, organize, synthesize, evaluate, and apply information about selected public issues —identifying, describing, and evaluating multiple points of view;
d. identify and practice selected forms of civic discussion and participation consistent with the ideals of citizens in a democratic republic;	d. practice forms of civic discussion and participation consistent with the ideals of citizens in a democratic republic;	d. practice forms of civic discussion and participation consistent with the ideals of citizens in a democratic republic;
e. explain actions citizens can take to influence public policy decisions;	e. explain and analyze various forms of citizen action that influence public policy decisions;	e. analyze and evaluate the influence of various forms of citizen action on public policy;
f. recognize that a variety of formal and informal actors influence and shape public policy;	f. identify and explain the roles of formal and informal political actors in influencing and shaping public policy and decision-making;	f. analyze a variety of public policies and issues from the perspective of formal and informal political actors;
g. examine the influence of public opinion on personal decision-making and government policy on public issues;	g. analyze the influence of diverse forms of public opinion on the development of public policy and decision-making;	g. evaluate the effectiveness of public opinion in influencing and shaping public policy development and decision-making;
h. explain how public policies and citizen behaviors may or may not reflect the stated ideals of a democratic republican form of government;	h. analyze the effectiveness of selected public policies and citizen behaviors in realizing the stated ideals of a democratic republican form of government;	h. evaluate the degree to which public policies and citizen behaviors reflect or foster the stated ideals of a democratic republican form of government;
i. describe how public policies are used to address issues of public concern;	i. explain the relationship between policy statements and action plans used to address issues of public concern;	i. construct a policy statement and an action plan to achieve one or more goals related to an issue of public concern;
j. recognize and interpret how the "common good" can be strengthened through various forms of citizen action.	j. examine strategies designed to strengthen the "common good," which consider a range of options for citizen action.	j. participate in activities to strengthen the "common good," based upon careful evaluation of possible options for citizen action.

Four STANDARDS INTO PRACTICE: EXAMPLES FOR THE EARLY GRADES

Early Grades  *Culture*

Social studies programs should include experiences that provide for the study of *culture and cultural diversity*, so that the learner can:

Performance Expectations   **Related Themes**

a. explore and describe similarities and differences in the ways groups, societies, and cultures address similar human needs and concerns;   **II III V**

b. give examples of how experiences may be interpreted differently by people from diverse cultural perspectives and frames of reference;   **II III IV V   IX**

c. describe ways in which language, stories, folktales, music, and artistic creations serve as expressions of culture and influence behavior of people living in a particular culture;   **II III V IX**

d. compare ways in which people from different cultures think about and deal with their physical environment and social conditions;   **II III V**

e. give examples and describe the importance of cultural unity and diversity within and across groups.   **II III V IX**

FOCUS ON THE CLASSROOM: STANDARDS INTO PRACTICE

Example #1
Performance Expectations: a, d

The first grade class has been studying families and has just finished creating a bulletin board entitled "Many Kinds of Families." Teacher Wilhelmina Tomashek has led the discussion about how families have changed and how many families today include members other than the mother, father, and children.

Tomashek then discusses family wants and needs and has students make a classroom book, using pictures they draw or cut out of magazines. The students relate these wants and needs to the environment/temperature/climate. They make a chart displaying wants and needs during cold and warm weather, which relates to the weather unit the students are doing in science. In group murals, students display what families might need and want in the future. The group murals will be assessed in terms of their responses to wants and needs related to natural environments.

Example #2
Performance Expectations: a, b, d

Carlene Jackson is an active member of her state's Geographic Alliance and enjoys participating in its institutes and staff development activities. This year she has worked with several primary teachers in her district to revise and improve the elementary social studies program. An ongoing concern of the intermediate teachers is the failure of students in the early grades to develop geography understanding. Jackson has volunteered to pilot the new program in her first grade class.

Before the first day of school, Jackson looks over her class list, inferring from the children's surnames that she will have students of Mexican, Vietnamese, and Korean ancestry. She also knows that, because of the general population of the school, she will have students of African-American and European-American backgrounds. This rich mix of cultural backgrounds provides Jackson with many opportunities to expose her students to experiences that increase their geographic knowledge and skills and their cultural understanding.

By the end of the first month of school, Jackson and her first graders decide to study and compare how families meet their basic needs of food, clothing, and shelter in their community, with how families meet their needs in Juarez, Mexico; Hanoi, Vietnam; Lagos, Nigeria; and Frankfurt, Germany. To do this, Jackson and the students create the following chart:

How Families Meet Basic Needs

Needs	Our City	Juarez	Hanoi	Lagos	Frankfurt
food					
shelter					
clothing					

Throughout the unit, Jackson and her students read books and stories, look at photos and slides, watch videos, and talk to speakers from their designated cities. The students sharpen their skills in reading, writing, and speaking, in addition to learning new geography skills such as basic map reading. For each city, they read and discuss something about its location, climate, region, and people.

By the end of the unit, Jackson's students can discuss how people in at least five different places meet their basic needs. Through students' discussion and formal writing, Jackson assesses the quality of student learning by determining if they are now more knowledgeable about how cultures meet similar needs, the ways in which societal needs are influenced by geographic characteristics, and the role of economic forces in determining how wants and needs are met.

⓪ *Time, Continuity, & Change*

Social studies programs should include experiences that provide for the study of *the ways human beings view themselves in and over time,* so that the learner can:

Performance Expectations	Related Themes
a. demonstrate an understanding that different people may describe the same event or situation in diverse ways, citing reasons for the differences in views;	Ⅰ Ⅲ Ⅳ Ⅴ
b. demonstrate an ability to use correctly vocabulary associated with time such as past, present, future, and long ago; read and construct simple timelines; identify examples of change; and recognize examples of cause and effect relationships;	Ⅰ Ⅲ Ⅴ Ⅷ
c. compare and contrast different stories or accounts about past events, people, places, or situations, identifying how they contribute to our understanding of the past;	Ⅰ Ⅲ Ⅹ
d. identify and use various sources for reconstructing the past, such as documents, letters, diaries, maps, textbooks, photos, and others;	Ⅰ Ⅲ
e. demonstrate an understanding that people in different times and places view the world differently;	Ⅰ Ⅲ Ⅸ
f. use knowledge of facts and concepts drawn from history, along with elements of historical inquiry, to inform decision-making about and action-taking on public issues.	Ⅰ Ⅲ Ⅴ Ⅵ Ⅶ Ⅷ Ⅸ Ⅹ

FOCUS ON THE CLASSROOM: STANDARDS INTO PRACTICE

Example #1

Performance Expectations: b, c, d, e

For the past three months, Leah Moulton's class of first, second, and third grade students has been studying their community, and they are now ready to take a closer look at its history. Moulton organizes the class into cooperative groups of four students each, and gives each group a copy of a historical photograph of their community.

Moulton tells the students: "We have read and talked a lot about our community. Photographs can help us learn much about its history. Study and discuss the photo I gave to your group. Appoint a recorder, and have the recorder write answers to the questions about the photos on your worksheets."

The students proceed to discuss the following:

1. What is the most important thing you saw in the photo?
2. Tell two things about the photo that surprised you.
3. Find and list two things in the photo that you might not see if the photo was taken today in our community.
4. Give the photo a title that accurately describes its contents.

Moulton then has the groups exchange photographs so that each photo is examined by a second group, which completes the same worksheet assignments. Some time later, she says: "Now that two groups have looked at the same photograph, the two groups that examined the same photo should sit together and share their worksheet responses. Be prepared to tell the class about your photo, and we'll then attempt to decide which photo is the oldest and why." The class spends the rest of the allotted time sharing observations. Toward the conclusion of the lesson, Moulton asks a spokesperson for each group to describe the photo and respond to the worksheet questions. She then engages the students in a discussion about which photo is the oldest and randomly selects students to justify their responses, based upon their large group sharing.

Later that week, Moulton organizes her class into pairs to complete an assessment activity. She says, "You and your partner will need to decide which of the following topics you want to illustrate: transportation, land use, schools, people, stores, or residences. After you decide on your topic, you will be responsible for completing two illustrations, one that shows your topic as it appears today in the present, and another as it appeared long ago in our community's past. Cooperatively decide in your pairs on a label for each of your illustrations, and then write a statement that contains an accurate description of the illustration topic and an accurate time reference." After students complete their illustrations, Moulton shares all of them with the class via a display on the classroom bulletin board, and invites parents to attend an after-school reception at which students explain how they created their illustrations.

Example #2
Performance Expectations: a, c, d, e

As part of their study of the Pacific Rim, the students in Edna Dillard's second/third grade class arrive with their homework assignment of a list of immigrants; their lists might include members of their family, friends, neighbors, etc. who have come from other countries to the United States. In pairs, they discuss their results and find the relevant countries on a globe. They then put push pins on a bulletin board map, showing where the immigrants were born; they attach to the pins small tags with the person's name. While waiting their turn, groups discuss why the people might have left their homeland, what they like about living in the United States, and if there is a pattern to the countries from which the people immigrated.

The next day, students read letters from immigrants in the community and from Dillard's relatives, which are provided them by the teacher. Dillard writes on the chalkboard two headings: "How the Immigrants Feel About Their Country of Birth" and "Immigrants' Impressions of the United States." The students discuss if the immigrants experience a sense of loss upon leaving their own cultures, along with surprises the immigrants found when they arrived in the United States. One family, for example, was surprised by the great number of automobiles at the airport where they landed. The range of immigrant experiences includes one immigrant who was adopted, another who had been interned in a refugee camp, and a third whose father had been transferred to the United States for business reasons.

The students want to know more about the family histories of the immigrants, and Dillard invites a series of immigrants to visit the class. These immigrants include people who have come during the past ten years, as well as some who arrived 30 to 50 years ago. Because this school is located in the Pacific Northwest, most of the immigrants are from Pacific Rim countries. The students work with Dillard to brainstorm interview questions, including reasons for immigrating, problems the immigrants encountered during their travels, the reception they received from residents upon arrival, changes they have experienced in their lives, aspects of their culture that they have retained, and other aspects they have changed.

The students interview the immigrants and develop presentations with charts focused on one or two aspects of each immigrant's experience. One group compares and contrasts the reasons for immigration; another, the problems encountered by the immigrants; another, the different feelings the immigrants have about their experiences; and so forth, with each group's findings summarized visually on a large chart. The groups present their findings to the entire class. Then, each group responds to questions posed by other students. Assessment will focus on clarity, accuracy of information, and credibility of students' findings when judged by the available evidence from the class interviews. At the end of the unit, all of the immigrants interviewed and their families are invited to the school for an evening program at which the student groups present their findings and the immigrants share other experiences with the students, their parents, and other members of the community.

Example #3
Performance Expectations: b, c, d

Luis Santos's fourth grade students are studying the Northeast region of the United States. As part of this study, the students are identifying people involved in major events associated with the Revolutionary War. Santos divides the class into six groups. He assigns each group of students a specific person (e.g., George III, Sam Frances, Elizabeth Freeman, Patrick Henry, Mercy Otis Warren, and George Washington) and asks them to develop scenes that highlight their character's contributions before, during, or after the Revolutionary War. He asks the students to establish the setting and a situation in which their character is taking the lead. Students use a variety of resource materials to assist in developing the setting and dialogue for their character and others involved in their scene.

After students develop their scenes, Santos asks them to determine the correct chronological order of the scenes and then to perform their scenes for their classmates. When all scenes have been performed, the class decides whether any additional narrator text is necessary to explain how the scenes are linked, in order to present the clearest and most accurate view of how the presentation content relates to the major events of the Revolutionary War period.

To evaluate the quality of the student performances, Santos and the students discuss these questions: Were the scenes portrayed in correct chronological order? Did each scene illustrate something important to the story? Did the scenes fit together so they told the story well? Was anything important left out? Were causes and effects clearly and accurately shown?

Ⅲ *People, Places, & Environments*

Social studies programs should include experiences that provide for the study of *people, places, and environments,* so that the learner can:

Performance Expectations	Related Themes
a. construct and use mental maps of locales, regions, and the world that demonstrate understanding of relative location, direction, size, and shape;	Ⅸ
b. interpret, use, and distinguish various representations of the earth, such as maps, globes, and photographs;	Ⅰ
c. use appropriate resources, data sources, and geographic tools such as atlases, data bases, grid systems, charts, graphs, and maps to generate, manipulate, and interpret information;	
d. estimate distance and calculate scale;	
e. locate and distinguish among varying landforms and geographic features, such as mountains, plateaus, islands, and oceans;	Ⅸ
f. describe and speculate about physical system changes, such as seasons, climate and weather, and the water cycle;	Ⅷ Ⅸ
g. describe how people create places that reflect ideas, personality, culture, and wants and needs as they design homes, playgrounds, classrooms, and the like;	Ⅰ Ⅳ Ⅴ
h. examine the interaction of human beings and their physical environment, the use of land, building of cities, and ecosystem changes in selected locales and regions;	Ⅵ Ⅷ
i. explore ways that the earth's physical features have changed over time in the local region and beyond and how these changes may be connected to one another;	Ⅱ Ⅸ
j. observe and speculate about social and economic effects of environmental changes and crises resulting from phenomena such as floods, storms, and drought;	Ⅰ Ⅴ Ⅶ
k. consider existing uses and propose and evaluate alternative uses of resources and land in home, school, community, the region, and beyond.	Ⅴ Ⅶ Ⅷ Ⅸ Ⅹ

FOCUS ON THE CLASSROOM: STANDARDS INTO PRACTICE

Example #1
Performance Expectations: a, b, g, h

As they come into class, the kindergarten children are very excited to find a large strip of paper going down the middle of the classroom floor. Their teacher, Jacob Stern, tells them to hang up their coats and come sit beside the paper strip. He tells them that the strip is a highway connecting two distant towns.

Stern takes a toy car and starts driving it along the highway. He tells the children that it takes several hours to get from one town to the other. He asks, "What might happen as someone drives along?" After much discussion, the children mention running out of gas, being hungry, getting tired. He then asks, "What services might be necessary for people as they drive from town to town?" The children respond with ideas such as gas stations, restaurants, and motels.

"Since you suggested it, Tanisha, would you like to own the gas station?" The child happily agrees, and Stern says, "This gas station will be Tanisha's Gas Station." He continues like this, using milk cartons for the various buildings needed.

Now, several decisions must be made by the children. Stern asks, "Where will you put your gas station and other services?" Tanisha decides the gas station should be near the highways so that the station can be seen by drivers and they can get to it easily. Tanisha wants her station to be Tanisha's Chevron Station. Stern writes the name on the station.

The next question is where Tanisha will live. Stern asks, "Do you want to live close to your business? Do you want to live near the highway? Do you want to be on the same side of the highway?" Tanisha puts her house behind the gas station.

The children now know the format for building the community, and many businesses and residences start developing. Miguel wants to open a restaurant and must decide whether it is to be a fast-food place or an expensive restaurant. Shoji wants to open a motel; Sarah, a grocery store.

After some of the needs of the highway travellers are met, the children will think about the needs of the people living in the community. Stern observes that individual children are able to cite specific community needs. As they contribute ideas about adding stores, schools, churches, banks, and a power company, the community grows in complexity.

Stern leads activities in which the community is named, decisions about streets and highways are made, and business problems are discussed. In small groups, the children draw maps of their community on large sheets of paper. As the students work at making decisions, Stern encourages them to think about the ways in which people's wants and needs influence the human-built environment. They talk about the ways in which these wants and needs influence the physical patterns of the emerging community. He is able to observe the accuracy with which the children express the relative locations, directions, and sizes of buildings on their maps. Over the course of several months, the children develop greater accuracy in their map-making and greater sophistication in the inferences they draw.

Example #2
Performance Expectations: a, b, c, d

As part of learning about their community, Ginny Adams's six- and seven-year-old students are working on developing mental maps of their city, including locations of major features and services. The Bureau of Tourism has provided colorful pictorial maps which students use to "explore" the city area by area. In addition, two parents of class members have created a large plastic floor outline map which contains only information necessary for orientation.

Each day, the children work with Adams in using the city maps. They discuss new areas of the city, reading the map to determine what features and services are found there. Children who have been to the area describe what they've seen.

After getting this overview of their city, the children cluster in small groups, and each group selects a different area for a study project. Working in groups, they create pop-up maps of their area and locate them accurately on the floor map. One group creates its pop-up of the zoo area. Another creates its pop-up of the community park, which includes the new pool complex. Yet another group creates representations of the downtown library and monuments.

To evaluate the accuracy of students' mental maps of the city, each student independently draws an outline map of the metropolitan area. On this outline, they draw major streets and landmarks and mark where their special pop-up area is located. Adams assesses the students' work for accuracy of the location of the pop-ups and the quality of presentation.

Example #3
Performance Expectations: a, b, d, g, h, k

The children in Tony Croce's multi-age primary classroom are gathered around pictures recently hung on the wall. The pictures are bird's eye views each child has drawn of his or her bedroom. This activity is part of an effort to help students develop greater understanding of scale. In addition, the children are examining how the places they live in have been designed and organized in ways that reflect the ideas, personalities, wants, and needs of various family members.

This is just one of many activities leading to a major class project: the design of a new school playground. The parent association and school district are working together on this project and want suggestions from children. The children have been developing a greater understanding of how human-designed spaces can meet the various needs of the users of those spaces.

With this background, the children divide into groups to research such things as: activities children want and need, equipment sensitive to special needs children, climate considerations, size and location of the playground, and costs. They bring their information together and, working as a class, they develop a set of recommendations for a specific playground design. Working in small groups, the students make models of their playground recommendations. Each model is assessed for its appropriateness of scale and representation of ideas. The class then selects one of the models and presents it to the PTA and student council. Following modifications, the class presents a final model to the school board, along with their reasons for the recommendations.

Ⅳ *Individual Development & Identity*

Social studies programs should include experiences that provide for the study of *individual development and identity*, so that the learner can:

Performance Expectations	**Related Themes**
a. describe personal changes over time, such as those related to physical development and personal interests;	**Ⅱ**
b. describe personal connections to place—especially place as associated with immediate surroundings;	**Ⅲ**
c. describe the unique features of one's nuclear and extended families;	**Ⅰ**
d. show how learning and physical development affect behavior;	
e. identify and describe ways family, groups, and community influence the individual's daily life and personal choices;	**Ⅰ** **Ⅴ**
f. explore factors that contribute to one's personal identity such as interests, capabilities, and perceptions;	
g. analyze a particular event to identify reasons individuals might respond to it in different ways;	**Ⅰ** **Ⅴ**
h. work independently and cooperatively to accomplish goals.	**Ⅹ**

FOCUS ON THE CLASSROOM: STANDARDS INTO PRACTICE

Example #1
Performance Expectations: a, e, h

Teacher Janis Johnson reads *Mirandy and Brother Wind* by Patricia McKissick to her second graders, concluding with the author's note about the photograph of her grandparents before they were married that had inspired the book. The terms "cakewalk" and "conjurer" are discussed.

Johnson asks, "Do you have any old photographs of your grandparents when they were young?" Most of the children are eager to tell about their photo albums. Johnson again asks, "Do you have anything that was owned by your parents or grandparents when they were young?" Again, positive responses. She says, "Tomorrow I would like you to share an artifact with us. Be sure to ask your parents about the story that goes with your artifact."

The next day students bring such objects as an ancient silver waffle iron, carved wooden eggs, salt and pepper shakers, newspapers, a yellow-handled spatula, and many old photographs. Students write stories about each artifact. As the stories are developing, students consider such questions as: How do you think the person who used this item felt? Why do you think the artifact was valued? Do you have something that will become an artifact? Explain why you think so. After typing, revising, and peer editing, the stories are published in a classroom book along with pictures drawn to go with the stories.

Johnson reads the stories to determine each student's understanding of the concept of artifact, the reasonableness of the inferences that students drew about the possible use of each artifact, and the logic of their inferences about future artifacts.

Example #2
Performance Expectations: a, b, g

One day in early September, Lorraine Lapsley takes her kindergarten class on a walk around the school. The children notice a beautiful dogwood tree they can see from their room, and they decide to "adopt" the tree—to appreciate it, observe it, and get to know it as a special tree. When they return to their classroom, each child paints a picture of the tree, and the class develops a story about it, how it looks this fall, and how they plan to watch this "friend" all year long.

The next day, the children are each weighed and measured. They record the measurements on a class chart, and each child draws a picture of himself or herself and writes the date on it.

About six weeks later, the children take another walk around the school, noticing all of the trees, but especially their "friend," the dogwood. The dogwood's leaves have changed color. The children take a few of the leaves back to their room, draw pictures of their tree, and develop another story that describes how the tree has changed. Lapsley reads aloud to the class Leo Buscaglia's *The Fall of Freddy the Leaf: A Story of Life for All Ages,* and the students discuss changes. They also draw pictures of themselves and date them to show how they have changed.

This process is repeated again at the end of the school year. By this time the children are able to draw final pictures of the tree and of themselves. Each child also writes a story about how each living thing is special and changes over time: their "friend," the dogwood tree, and themselves. The teacher examines each child's series of pictures and final story to assess each's understanding of change. The pictures and stories become part of the work each child will take along to his or her first grade teacher.

Example #3
Performance Expectations: e, g, h

Jan Gonzales has been reading stories to her third grade class. The stories include characters who see the same situation differently for a variety of reasons. The children have noticed and discussed the fact that the characters form their ideas about the situation based on their own experiences, beliefs, and attitudes. The class has also been studying the way U.S. courts work and has discussed how different witnesses sometimes see the same situation differently.

Now Gonzales gives the students a copy of a news photo that has several unfamiliar characters and is open to interpretation as to exactly what is happening. After each student has had a reasonable amount of time to examine the photo, it is removed from view and each child writes a description entitled "What I Saw." Gonzales emphasizes writing statements that the children are prepared to defend (as a witness would "under oath"); these would be statements of what the children believe actually happened in the news photo they observed.

Once each child has completed his or her written interpretation, students move into groups of five or six and share their written descriptions. They take note of the differences they hear from one "witness's" version to another's.

The children then prepare individual written statements, describing two or three discrepancies noted among the accounts offered in their group and explaining why they believe the discrepancies may have occurred. Criteria for evaluation include the child's ability to recognize and describe differences, suggest causes, and recognize that the way an individual views an incident reflects personal beliefs, experiences, and attitudes.

Gonzales plans a follow-up discussion to encourage the children to learn from each other's written responses and to ensure that the children understand how this lesson relates to the differing assumptions illustrated by the story she read to the class earlier.

Ⓥ *Individuals, Groups, & Institutions*

Social studies programs should include experiences that provide for the study of *interactions among individuals, groups, and institutions,* so that the learner can:

Performance Expectations   **Related Themes**

a. identify roles as learned behavior patterns in group situations such as student, family member, peer play group member, or club member;   Ⓘ Ⓥ

b. give examples of and explain group and institutional influences such as religious beliefs, laws, and peer pressure, on people, events, and elements of culture;   Ⓘ Ⓘ Ⓥ Ⓥ
Ⓧ

c. identify examples of institutions and describe the interactions of people with institutions;   Ⓘ Ⓥ Ⓧ

d. identify and describe examples of tensions between and among individuals, groups, or institutions, and how belonging to more than one group can cause internal conflicts;   Ⓘ Ⓘ Ⓥ Ⓧ

e. identify and describe examples of tension between an individual's beliefs and government policies and laws;   Ⓘ Ⓥ Ⓥ Ⓧ

f. give examples of the role of institutions in furthering both continuity and change;   Ⓘ Ⓥ Ⓥ Ⓧ

g. show how groups and institutions work to meet individual needs and promote the common good, and identify examples of where they fail to do so.   Ⓘ Ⓘ Ⓥ Ⓧ

FOCUS ON THE CLASSROOM: STANDARDS INTO PRACTICE

Example #1
Performance Expectations: c, f, g

Phyllis Jett's second grade students brainstorm issues of concern within their community. Working in small groups, they choose one issue they wish to address. With Jett's assistance, the groups investigate whether there are organizations within the community that target this concern and determine recent activities they have undertaken. One group that had selected child abuse as a concern discovers that Micro City Government, an African-American student service organization, recently canvassed their neighborhoods to identify "SAFE" homes children can go to when they are frightened and in need of adult help.

Students bring the information they have gathered back to the class. The class then selects three or four organizations in whose efforts they are particularly interested. Working in groups, they develop proposals to present to these organizations, suggesting ways the children think they can contribute to these efforts. The proposals are sent to the organizations in the hope that one or more community service efforts can be undertaken.

Students keep individual journals of their activities during the process described above and the efforts that follow in which they become personally involved. Journals reflect actions taken as well as the children's personal responses to those actions. Clarity, thoroughness, and accurate information in journal entries serve as criteria for Jett to evaluate evidence of growing knowledge and interest in community service.

Early Grades

Example #2

Performance Expectations: a, b

To provide students the opportunity to examine roles in various societies, Clarice Mean introduces her third grade students to the societies of an ant farm and a beehive. Using a live ant farm, films, CD-ROM, and other resources on the honey bee, she lets her students examine the various roles of the ants and bees and then assists them in transferring this knowledge to their own lives in a human society. After the insect investigation, the students make lists showing roles of the members of the ant and bee colonies. The students then generate lists of how their roles as students compare and contrast with those of the insects.

To assess whether the students understand the concept of roles, Mean presents a situation. She tells the class, "On Thursday we are going to an assembly given by a touring opera company. What will be your role during the assembly? How can you most effectively perform your role?"

Following the assembly and discussion of the roles seen there, Mean has her students brainstorm other situations in which they have a particular role to perform and has them write about how they would effectively do so. These writings are shared in small groups for further discussion.

Mean furthers this study of roles by focusing on changing roles: i.e., how and why they change. Her students examine how roles change in adulthood as individuals become workers, parents, volunteers, and grandparents. She frequently uses role-plays to place children into various roles and help them to self-examine changes in behavior, attitudes, and goals as the roles vary. Finally, she has students examine how the notion of conformity plays an important part in the ways they determine certain roles should be played.

Mean keeps running records of how well her students are able to articulate their understanding of the function and importance of roles in various situations and how roles change depending on expectations and changing conditions. She uses her running records to help her talk with parents about their children's progress in social studies.

Example #3

Performance Expectations: b, d, e, g

Singer Marian Anderson's voice could be heard coming from Donna Ognebene's fourth grade classroom. Once the students are in their seats, Ognebene tells them about Marian Anderson's early life. She has the students listen especially for the obstacles Anderson had to overcome and how she did so. The students identify laws and customs in society that, at that time, made it difficult for an African-American woman to have her talents acknowledged. They also identify how Anderson was able to succeed and to help change some of the customs that had been obstacles for her.

In pairs, the students then research Jackie Robinson, Martin Luther King, Jr., Sacajawea, Amelia Earhart, Nelson Mandela, Tecumseh, Mother Clara Hall, and Franklin Chang-Dias. They look for obstacles each person had to overcome and how each dealt with those obstacles. Ognebene has her students prepare posters depicting the information they found about each person and then share it with the class. As students listen and question their peers, they look for common characteristics and obstacles these individuals had to face. They discover that often beliefs and customs held by certain groups can help or hurt people as they strive to use their talents. They also find that sometimes individuals can change those beliefs and customs in ways that will help people in the future succeed more easily.

Ognebene evaluates the poster displays, using the criteria of accuracy, power of visual images, and clarity of organization in presenting information.

Ⓥ *Power, Authority, & Governance*

Social studies programs should include experiences that provide for the study of *how people create and change structures of power, authority, and governance,* so that the learner can:

Performance Expectations   **Related Themes**

a. examine the rights and responsibilities of the individual in relation to his or her social group, such as family, peer group, and school class;   ⓥ ⓧ

b. explain the purpose of government;   ⓧ

c. give examples of how government does or does not provide for needs and wants of people, establish order and security, and manage conflict;   Ⓘ ⓥ ⓘⅹ

d. recognize how groups and organizations encourage unity and deal with diversity to maintain order and security;   Ⓘ ⓥ

e. distinguish among local, state, and national government and identify representative leaders at these levels such as mayor, governor, and president;   ⓧ

f. identify and describe factors that contribute to cooperation and cause disputes within and among groups and nations;   Ⅱ ⓥ ⓘⅹ

g. explore the role of technology in communications, transportation, information-processing, weapons development, or other areas as it contributes to or helps resolve conflicts;   Ⅶ Ⅷ ⓘⅹ

h. recognize and give examples of the tensions between the wants and needs of individuals and groups, and concepts such as fairness, equity, and justice.   Ⅱ ⓘⅹ ⓧ

FOCUS ON THE CLASSROOM: STANDARDS INTO PRACTICE

Example #1
Performance Expectations: a, b, c, f, h

Using the story line method, Grace Anne Heacock's third grade class has established a town they have named Countervail, in which each student has created a family, its house, and collectively a rather complex community. The bulletin board display of the town now extends along walls and tables, and students have become quite involved in the goings-on in Countervail. To the children's dismay, however, they discover one morning that there is trash in their park and graffiti scratched on fences. One family's rabbit is missing, and the new tree in front of the plaza has been cut down.

The students have come face to face with the need for laws; otherwise, nothing can be done to stop this destruction of "their" property. For the next week, students work in cooperative groups, each dealing with a different set of concerns, to begin the process of developing a legal code for the community of Countervail.

The students brainstorm with Heacock the problems created by the property destruction and suggest a list of "do's" and "don'ts" for Countervail's population. Reviewing the list, students develop ideas about what is acceptable and unacceptable behavior. They examine a set of laws in their actual town that Heacock has rewritten in simplified form, and then identify those that appear to be relevant to their case.

Heacock invites their actual town's mayor, police chief, and fire chief to visit the class. Each guest reviews the relevant laws and discusses them with the students. The students gather information from each guest and construct charts indicating responsibilities citizens in Countervail assume for each proposed law.

As a culminating activity, Heacock has students prepare a "charter of laws" for Countervail. This charter is then shared with local officials and experts on the law, who are asked to write letters or prepare videotaped responses to the student charter. The students review the adult responses and prepare journal entries about the significance of law and its importance in the community. Heacock evaluates the quality of the journal entries based upon the clarity of student language, use of examples from the case study, and inclusion of reactions to the adult responses to the student charter.

Example #2
Performance Expectations: b

Tarry Lindquist's fourth grade class has been discussing different forms of government: democracy, monarchy, military dictatorship, and anarchy. In their home groups, each student has become the expert in one form of government through his or her jigsaw cooperative learning group. Lindquist then gives them an unusual assignment: bring in lots of clear plastic cups of different sizes. She asks those students whose parents are in the medical professions to bring in the little cups that hospitals use to give patients their pills. She also scurries around gathering up an assortment of clear plastic cups and a clear pitcher for each group. She mixes up a batch of colored water for each group. Lindquist tells each group that the colored liquid is power, and asks each group to divide up the power to show each of their kinds of government. Of course, she talks about being careful in pouring and cleaning up. As students work on solving the problem, she visits each group around the room, giving hints and asking questions. The next day, students show their solutions to the problem to the class and explain why they made the choices they did.

As each group justifies its choice, Lindquist has the rest of the students gather information from their peers and create a chart containing categories based upon the different forms of government. Each group then identifies and explains at least two distinctions between their assigned form of government and others that were studied.

At the conclusion of the discussion of comparisons and contrasts, Lindquist distributes a set of four paragraphs describing hypothetical situations illustrative of the four different forms of government under study. Each student individually labels the descriptions as a democracy, monarchy, military dictatorship, or anarchy, and then justifies his or her decision in essay form. Lindquist has the students exchange their written responses to discuss the individual justifications in small groups. Each student receives two critiques of his or her justification using a process of peer review before Lindquist collects the final assignment, which students can revise based upon the peer review if they choose.

Criteria for evaluation of quality include use of cogent reasons, application of relevant examples from classwork, and development of an argument, citing appropriate characteristics for each form of government.

ⓥ *Production, Distribution, & Consumption*

Social studies programs should include experiences that provide for the study of *how people organize for the production, distribution, and consumption of goods and services*, so that the learner can:

Performance Expectations	Related Themes
a. give examples that show how scarcity and choice govern our economic decisions;	I III
b. distinguish between needs and wants;	IV
c. identify examples of private and public goods and services;	V VI
d. give examples of the various institutions that make up economic systems such as families, workers, banks, labor unions, government agencies, small businesses, and large corporations;	V
e. describe how we depend upon workers with specialized jobs and the ways in which they contribute to the production and exchange of goods and services;	V VIII
f. describe the influence of incentives, values, traditions, and habits on economic decisions;	I II
g. explain and demonstrate the role of money in everyday life;	I
h. describe the relationship of price to supply and demand;	I V
i. use economic concepts such as supply, demand, and price to help explain events in the community and nation;	I V VI
j. apply knowledge of economic concepts in developing a response to a current local economic issue, such as how to reduce the flow of trash into a rapidly filling landfill.	V VI VIII X

FOCUS ON THE CLASSROOM: STANDARDS INTO PRACTICE

Example #1

Performance Expectations: e, i

At the beginning of a unit on economic specialization in production, Mark Moran's early primary class is divided into two teams of cookie makers. Both teams make gingerbread cookies. One team works as an assembly line, each person having a special job—rolling out the dough, cutting the basic shape, making the almond mouth, locating raisin buttons, etc. The second team works as individuals, each person creating his or her own gingerbread cookies. Both teams have the same supplies to work with.

After they have finished baking their cookies, the students examine the cookies and identify the advantages and disadvantages of each method of producing cookies. Ideas that emerge relate to division of labor, pride, creativity, independence, specialization, and quality control.

Students subsequently prepare summaries in writing about how they produced their cookies. Moran evaluates the quality of the student writing by determining how accurate the students are in detailing the production process and the extent to which evidence of key concepts is present.

In the weeks that follow this lesson, students examine other situations involving assembly line production, including a field trip to a local plant where pickup trucks are assembled.

Early Grades

Example #2
Performance Expectations: a, h

Pete Vlahos introduces his fourth graders to concepts of trade and economic interdependence, using the newspaper and a weekly current events program. To demonstrate the complexities and issues surrounding international trade, he divides the class into seven groups, explaining that each group represents a country, each of which is about to build a new structure to house its government. This structure will be made using materials common in the classroom.

Each country group is given a large bag with supplies, tasks, and discussion sheets. When the groups take out the supplies allocated to them, they find that other groups have more, fewer, or different supplies than they have. One group registers its frustration with having only a bottle of glue and a pair of scissors. This group soon learns, however, that these commodities are in great demand and, through some savvy trading, the students are able to acquire ample supplies. It takes quite a while for each group to design its structure and acquire needed materials, but implementing effective trading strategies is the ultimate measure of success.

Upon completion of the task, the groups reconvene as a class, and students discuss how they felt when they saw the disparities in resources from one country to another, what problems they encountered in trading, how this activity mirrors the real world, and how trading helps or hinders countries. Vlahos evaluates the success of the lesson by asking students to provide other examples of how our economic system is connected to or dependent upon other countries.

Ⅷ *Science, Technology, & Society*

Social studies programs should include experiences that provide for the study of *relationships among science, technology, and society,* so that the learner can:

Performance Expectations   **Related Themes**

a. identify and describe examples in which science and technology have changed the lives   Ⅰ Ⅱ Ⅴ Ⅶ
of people, such as in homemaking, childcare, work, transportation, and communication;   Ⅸ

b. identify and describe examples in which science and technology have led to changes in   Ⅲ
the physical environment, such as the building of dams and levees, offshore oil drilling,
medicine from rain forests, and loss of rain forests due to extraction of resources or alternative
uses;

c. describe instances in which changes in values, beliefs, and attitudes have resulted from   Ⅰ Ⅱ Ⅴ Ⅵ
new scientific and technological knowledge, such as conservation of resources and awareness   Ⅶ Ⅸ Ⅹ
of chemicals harmful to life and the environment;

d. identify examples of laws and policies that govern scientific and technological applications,   Ⅵ Ⅹ
such as the Endangered Species Act and environmental protection policies;

e. suggest ways to monitor science and technology in order to protect the physical environment,   Ⅵ Ⅹ
individual rights, and the common good.

FOCUS ON THE CLASSROOM: STANDARDS INTO PRACTICE

Example #1
Performance Expectations: a, b, c, e

The third graders in Dodie Righi's class have established the need to study how humans change the environment. One of the issues being discussed is recycling. At lunch, one of the students, Jorge, notices that the cafeteria is serving juice in styrofoam cups. Since the students have learned that styrofoam requires the use of CFCs in the production process and that CFCs have a deleterious effect on the ozone layer, he goes to his teacher to express his concern.

Righi had been getting the class ready to take action on an environmental problem in the community, and Jorge's plea was a perfect teachable moment. While students discuss how to proceed in their cooperative learning groups, Mattie scoots to the cafeteria and copies down the address of the company that manufactures the cups. By the time Mattie returns, the groups are ready to report. Righi jots down their ideas on the overhead, and each group makes out a plan based on the ideas of the whole class. The students agree upon a plan that includes contacting the company to ask why they make cups of styrofoam and how many CFCs are released in the production of each cup. They next want to find out how many styrofoam cups the school uses annually; then, they can multiply and figure out how many CFCs are released into the air as a result of the use of styrofoam cups in their cafeteria. Righi asks each student to begin keeping a folder in which he or she maintains a record of the class's work on the problem.

Righi works with the students to plan how to make phone calls to businesses to get information effectively and how to write a business letter. After obtaining information, the students graph their data to show the impact of the styrofoam cups they consumed. The students use an electronic bulletin board to gather additional information, as well as CD-ROMs in the school media center and the local library to get more information on the manufacture of styrofoam.

When they have gathered enough information, the class discusses what they should do about it. Righi suggests that they explore alternatives to using the styrofoam cups. They go through the same information-gathering process, checking out paper cups and the feasibility of using their own cups and leaving them in their cubbies. The latter means that they need to talk with the Director of Public Health to find out about health standards. She explains to them the temperature at which they need to wash their own cups and the energy needed to purify, pump, and heat that water.

After looking at all the information, the students decide that the best solution is to use paper, rather than styrofoam, cups for snacks and lunches. The head of the cafeteria says that she needs a directive from the school board to make the change. With Righi's help, Roger calls the school board secretary and secures a spot on the agenda for the next meeting. For that week, the students work very hard in selecting the information they want to give the board and the visuals they want to show. The students prepare a videotape to use in an assembly program they present to the whole school and later to the board. They explain their efforts and analyze how their work can serve as a model for other student action strategies.

Righi evaluates their presentation on the clarity with which they represented the strategies and their ability to critique strategies for effectiveness. She also asks students to hand in their folders containing their record of all class activities related to this problem. She evaluates the folders on completeness of information, spelling, and grammar. She makes special notes on how well each student captures the nature of the problem on which the class worked, i.e., how various choices people make have different effects on the environment.

After the presentation to the school board, the board votes to switch to paper cups. Buoyed by their success, the students make the same presentation to the town council in an effort to get them to use paper cups in government offices.

Example #2

Performance Expectations: a, b, h

As part of a year-long study of their community, Marge Allender's second graders list important inventions, such as the automobile and television, and favorite activities, such as going to the zoo and sleeping over at a friend's house. Then, they match up the inventions that are necessary to carry out favorite activities and create a rebus in which pictures substitute for the inventions and activities. These become statements of the interdependence between technology and lifestyles, as in "If I didn't have a _____, I couldn't _____." These are written on sentence strips and displayed with the drawings to spark further discussion about lifestyle changes over time.

With Allender's help, students calculate the time it would take a horse-drawn vehicle

Early Grades to take them to a favorite field trip destination. They get there and back by school bus within a single school day. Could they have done so a hundred years ago? Using early maps of and information about the region, students suggest what might have substituted for today's field trips that would have been within walking distance and would be interesting and educational for children of the 1890s.

To bring the students into the present and get them thinking about the future, Allender has the students help her plan their actual field trip to the museum. They list the technical advancements that are necessary to make the trip, such as the bus, roads, and buildings. They draw pictures for each and place them on their growing display of their community. The next step is for small groups to decide where children would go on a field trip 20 years from now. Allender evaluates each student's "statement of interdependence" and drawing for appropriateness to the main ideas of the topic.

Ⅸ *Global Connections*

Social studies programs should include experiences that provide for the study of *global connections and interdependence*, so that the learner can:

Performance Expectations	Related Themes
a. explore ways that language, art, music, belief systems, and other cultural elements may facilitate global understanding or lead to misunderstanding;	Ⅰ Ⅲ
b. give examples of conflict, cooperation, and interdependence among individuals, groups, and nations;	Ⅴ Ⅵ
c. examine the effects of changing technologies on the global community;	Ⅷ
d. explore causes, consequences, and possible solutions to persistent, contemporary, and emerging global issues, such as pollution and endangered species;	Ⅲ Ⅷ
e. examine the relationships and tensions between personal wants and needs and various global concerns, such as use of imported oil, land use, and environmental protection;	Ⅳ Ⅶ Ⅷ
f. investigate concerns, issues, standards, and conflicts related to universal human rights, such as the treatment of children, religious groups, and effects of war.	Ⅹ

FOCUS ON THE CLASSROOM: STANDARDS INTO PRACTICE

Example #1
Performance Expectations: d, e, f

For their heritage unit, the children in Deanna Parker's combined first and second grade class interview their parents, grandparents, and relatives to find out what country or region their family may have emigrated from and when. They ask their relatives what they know about the family's former homeland and what it was like when the family left it for the United States. Those students who are unable to identify an original homeland are asked to join with another child who has. They create maps indicating their families' places of origin and movements over time, and gather additional information from library and other resources about the cultural heritage of the homeland.

As the year progresses, students gather news stories about the country or region of their heritage to learn about ways it has changed. Parker gives special emphasis to similarities and differences of the regions or countries with the United States and also emphasizes problems and issues facing these countries, helping the children understand the relationship between these and problems and issues faced in the United States and how each country deals with these concerns.

As a culmination activity, students working individually or in groups build a desktop museum to exhibit information they have gathered about the region or country of their ancestors. The librarian/media specialist and art and music teachers assist students with gathering arts resources and adding artistic touches to exhibits. Parents and other volunteers are invited to help in this project. Parents, relatives, special guests, and other students are invited to a schoolwide open house to view the exhibits.

Early Grades

Example #2
Performance Expectations: a

Landra Mitchell has collected artifacts from various countries and cultures around the world. Every time she hears of a colleague or friend planning a trip or an international student at the local university returning home for a vacation, she asks that they bring back an interesting artifact—a toy, a utensil, a newspaper, a coin, or any small, inexpensive item—to add to her collection.

During her "Going Global" thematic unit, she organizes a museum as a learning center. With this, her third and fourth year primary students examine a few artifacts a day, responding in writing to audiotaped prompts related to each one. Their responses create a "Going Global" journal of observations which become part of their assessment portfolio for the unit. Another way in which Mitchell assesses students' growing recognition of global connections is by having students respond to the following prompt: "Manuel Yanes has written a letter to you. He is from Venezuela and got your name from his teacher through an international penpal organization. Manuel tells you a great deal about himself, including that his favorite sport is 'futbol.' He also sends several photographs, one of which is a team holding a soccer ball. He has written on the back of the photo, 'My futbol team.' Use your research skills to find out as much as you can about Venezuela, its language, and the term 'futbol.' Then write back to Manuel and share with him what you have learned and the term we use for 'futbol.' Include in your letter additional information you think he might like to know about you and your country."

Criteria for evaluation include whether students used effective research strategies, clarity of explanation, interest level of additional topics selected for inclusion in the letter, and overall quality of the letter.

Example #3
Performance Expectations: b, d

The student council at Enatai Elementary decides to have "Save the Earth" as their year-long school theme. Critical to addressing this theme are lessons early on that help students realize that no one individual or group or country can save the earth alone in the school year but that saving the earth will take effort on everyone's part in their own corner of the world. Thus, the students of Enatai determine ways in which they can save their little piece of the earth.

The children brainstorm a list of activities and send a letter to each class in the school inviting them to choose one of the following in which to participate: clean the playground and neighborhood of litter; place recycling boxes in each classroom and office area; hold a newspaper and aluminum drive and send proceeds to an organization for preserving endangered species; develop ways to use fewer disposables in the cafeteria and ways to reduce the amount of waste that ends up in the dumpster; identify ways to reuse materials; write save-the-earth campaign letters for the school and community newspapers; or write to local hotels and motels requesting that they place recycling bins next to soda machines for aluminum recycling.

Ray Johnson's third grade class chooses the recycling box project. Students accumulate a number of extra large boxes and decide where they will be most useful. They then determine which boxes need liners to protect them from liquid waste. They soon find themselves faced with the dilemma of how to line a large box with a waterproof material. Large plastic bags, although creating some concern for the new environmentalists of Enatai, become the solution of choice. The children develop slogans and symbols to paint on the boxes to dress them up and help remind students to use them. The students share their idea and its success with their penpal class in Brazil and ask what their Brazilian friends are doing in their community to save their little corner of the earth.

At the end of the year, the Enatai projects become the topic of a special edition of the community newsletter the student council produces. Each class prepares a description and evaluation of its project and how it could be more successful, given recommended changes.

Ⓧ *Civic Ideals & Practices*

Social studies programs should include experiences that provide for the study of *the ideals, principles, and practices of citizenship in a democratic republic,* so that the learner can:

Performance Expectations   **Related Themes**

a. identify key ideals of the United States' democratic republican form of government, such as individual human dignity, liberty, justice, equality, and the rule of law, and discuss their application in specific situations; ⬤II ⬤V ⬤VI

b. identify examples of rights and responsibilities of citizens; ⬤II

c. locate, access, organize, and apply information about an issue of public concern from multiple points of view; ⬤I ⬤II ⬤V ⬤IX

d. identify and practice selected forms of civic discussion and participation consistent with the ideals of citizens in a democratic republic; ⬤II ⬤V ⬤VI

e. explain actions citizens can take to influence public policy decisions; ⬤V ⬤VI

f. recognize that a variety of formal and informal actors influence and shape public policy; ⬤V ⬤VI

g. examine the influence of public opinion on personal decision-making and government policy on public issues; ⬤V ⬤VI

h. explain how public policies and citizen behaviors may or may not reflect the stated ideals of a democratic republican form of government; ⬤II ⬤V ⬤VI

i. describe how public policies are used to address issues of public concern; ⬤VI

j. recognize and interpret how the "common good" can be strengthened through various forms of citizen action. ⬤II ⬤V ⬤VI

FOCUS ON THE CLASSROOM: STANDARDS INTO PRACTICE

Example #1
Performance Expectations: b, c, d, e

"Do you know that the school board wants to put a daycare center and preschool at our school? I don't want babies in my school! I heard that they are going to put daycare/preschools in every elementary school."

These are the views of a third grader, as representatives from each grade gather for the weekly student council meeting at Wilburton Elementary School. Sandra Roberts, the council advisor, expands the agenda to include this topic as the council discusses the rumors. The students don't all agree that having the little ones would be bad, but everyone does agree that they do not have enough information and need the answers to several questions. They begin to compile a list of questions: Where would the daycare center be housed? What would happen if the children got sick? Would they use school supplies? What if they were too noisy? Where would they play? Would they cause too much extra work? Might it be fun to have them?

The students invite the principal, Ann Peterson, to the next meeting to answer their questions. Meanwhile, they decide to return to their classes and generate more questions to ask at the next meeting and to begin to gather information to answer the ones they had already raised.

When they meet next, the principal answers many questions. She mentions that there is going to be a school board meeting on the issue in two weeks. The council decides to discuss the pros and cons and put them in a survey for other students. They also decide to develop a report that will provide background information and show the results of the student survey. Roberts and the children discuss what will be needed in the report. The children decide it should say what the problem is, present several opinions that groups of people hold, and show the results of the survey.

The student council officers and their parents arrive at the school board meeting with a chart to show all the steps they had taken to develop the report. They distribute copies of their report, which contains background on the issue, present pros and cons, and include a graph of the student survey results. The report details the cost of supplies and help needed for the center. It also indicates that many parents could be helped by such a center and that having more little children in elementary schools might make the other children feel more responsible. Older children might even enjoy reading stories to the little ones. Space for the center is still a concern at Wilburton. The report points out that a portable classroom will be needed if a center is added at Wilburton. Roberts is pleased that the report addresses all of the topics the children have suggested and that it is accurate.

The school board president passes out the report and tells the board members that the students at Wilburton Elementary School have been concerned about issues of housing, safety, and health related to the planned daycare/preschool centers. She urges committee members to listen to the students as they report and to use the information in the report to think about the decisions they will make. After listening to the students, the school board decides to discuss the matter and make a final decision at the next meeting.

At the next meeting, the school board votes to place a center in those elementary schools that have room and if they are in locations where a private daycare/preschool is not available. They also decide to invite businesses to consider making space available for centers to meet the needs of employees. The president of the school board congratulates the students for their excellent questions and for helping the committee to think about the many pros and cons of the proposal. The board urges the student council members to continue their good work aimed at studying and reporting on issues important to them and to their school.

Example #2
Performance Expectations: a, c, d, e, i, j

Ellen Stein's fourth grade class is studying how its local community government operates to solve problems of public concern. Their school is located next to an abandoned factory, which is being considered as a site for either a shopping center or a public park. Citizens holding different perspectives have argued and debated the merits of the two proposals in the media, and many of the students' parents have strong opinions about the issue. Because of the local concerns, the students want to study the issue, gather information, think about the consequences of different positions, and make their opinions heard.

Stein invites representatives from different groups in the community who will influence the decision to talk with students. People invited are the mayor, members of the planning board, the town council, the chamber of commerce, various citizens' groups, and a number of residents who live in the surrounding neighborhood. For each visit, small groups of students in the class are designated as information gatherers, recorders of answers to questions, and questioners. After the visits, students examine the positions of the different groups, and the class develops a list of questions, issues, and concerns to be sent along with "thank you" letters to the visitors. The students also discuss what each community group's priorities appear to be and how their community may be affected by the differing priorities of the groups.

After further information gathering and review of the pros and cons of several alternatives, the class decides to prepare a poster campaign, supporting the alternatives it believes are most beneficial for the interests of the entire community. Stern helps the students consider the elements that make effective posters: attention-grabbing qualities, visuals, wording that conveys a clear message, accuracy, evidence supporting the position presented, and persuasiveness. After developing their individual posters, students select the best poster using the qualities previously identified. Students invite the local newspaper to send a reporter and photographer to see the poster display in their school, take photos, and write an article. They also obtain permission to place the display in the regional library.

Five STANDARDS INTO PRACTICE: EXAMPLES FOR THE MIDDLE GRADES

 *Middle Grades*

 **I** *Culture*

Social studies programs should include experiences that provide for the study of *culture and cultural diversity*, so that the learner can:

Performance Expectations	Related Themes

a. compare similarities and differences in the ways groups, societies, and cultures meet human needs and concerns;   **II III V**

b. explain how information and experiences may be interpreted by people from diverse cultural perspectives and frames of reference;   **II III IV V IX**

c. explain and give examples of how language, literature, the arts, architecture, other artifacts, traditions, beliefs, values, and behaviors contribute to the development and transmission of culture;   **II III V IX**

d. explain why individuals and groups respond differently to their physical and social environments and/or changes to them on the basis of shared assumptions, values, and beliefs;   **II III V**

e. articulate the implications of cultural diversity, as well as cohesion, within and across groups.   **II III V IX**

FOCUS ON THE CLASSROOM: STANDARDS INTO PRACTICE

Example #1
Performance Expectations: a, c, d, e

The fifth grade students in Rose Sudmeier's class are sharing the stories behind their names in small groups. In constructing a "native culture" in their classroom, they have studied the place/environment, including descriptions, vocabulary development, visual presentations, and survival in the environment. This process led to a look at the people living in that place. They are now talking about naming traditions in general and how they came to be named.

The class researches the tools, food, and other survival necessities that would be needed in their place. They then begin to discuss what the people might do at night when it was dark or during the day when work was done and how traditions, such as the naming tradition, might be passed on. At this point, Sudmeier brings in her colleague, Dave Trowbridge, and his geography class from the high school, which has been studying traditions, storytelling, art, and music of the Northwest Coastal Indian tribes.

The high school students visit the fifth grade class on two different days, showing the elementary students how to do basic dance steps and how to make dancing masks. They also tell them stories of various legends and play musical tapes. The fifth graders continue their study for another three days on their own. The high school students plan a return visit for the end of the week, when they also invite the fifth graders to be their guests in a potlatch. At the potlatch, the high schoolers entertain the fifth graders with stories and then have them join them in dances and use the masks they had shown them how to make. In keeping with the potlatch tradition, the guests receive small gifts from the high school students at the end.

As an evaluation tool, Sudmeier has the children keep journals in which they write about their culture, traditions they started, poetry they wrote about their environment, and reflections on their participation in the various activities. She looks for the journals to be thoughtfully written, expressing positive views, accurate in the information presented, creative, and reflective.

Example #2
Performance Expectations: a, b, c, d, e

Near the end of the year, John Parker's seventh grade world studies class is studying Australia. They begin the unit by using multiple maps to identify physical and cultural patterns in Australia today. Student groups hypothesize reasons for population distribution patterns. Their hypotheses tend to explain contemporary cultural patterns in terms of environmental determinism; that is, people live the way that they do because the natural-physical environment requires them to live in those ways in order to survive, given the resources, climate, and the natural terrain.

After briefly sharing their hypotheses, students turn to their textbook chapter on Australia to find information that might support or suggest changes in their hypotheses. One or two students in each group add to the group's information by using more sophisticated reference sources, while one or two students use picture books to add visual evidence.

The groups review and revise their hypotheses on the basis of their findings and then view a video dealing with traditional aboriginal lifeways in the Australian outback. Parker says to the class, "O.K., you said people live the way they do in Australia because of the physical-natural environment. If that is true, why did the aboriginal people who were there when the Europeans arrived live in such a different way in the very same natural environment?"

Student groups develop cultural explanations to account for these differences. The groups then share their explanations. Some emphasize belief systems; others explain the differences in terms of learned behavior patterns. After thorough discussion, students apply the basic concept of culture as the motivation for behavior. Each student writes a paragraph presenting his or her best explanation for the difference in the ways of contemporary Australians and aboriginal peoples.

Example #3
Performance Expectations: a, b, c, e

Chanda Winston's eighth grade students are studying the Americans before European contact. One student, Benjamin Whitehorse, remarks that the class used the term "Indian" in such a general way that it suggested no difference among the many tribes that inhabited the continent. "You're right," says Winston. "While I'm sure you have heard of many different tribes and recognize that a variety of factors shaped their group norms, customs, and traditions, it is easy for us to forget and begin talking in generalities. Let's do something about that."

At their next class session, Winston paraphrases her discussion with Benjamin and passes out a copy of the poem "On the Pulse of Morning," written and read by Maya Angelou at the 1993 Clinton Presidential Inauguration. She draws their attention to the section that reads, "You, who gave me my first name, you Pawnee, Apache, Seneca, you Cherokee nation."

"Why do you think the poet named these Indian groups separately? Why didn't she just say Indians?" asks Winston. The students suggest a variety of reasons including the poet's attempt to recognize American Indians as distinct cultural groups and the use of listing as a literary device.

Winston then lists on the board the four groups that were mentioned in the poem and adds the Arawak, whom Columbus first encountered. She divides the students into groups to research general questions about the groups: their geographic regions, what we know about them before European contact, what we know about them after European contact, and what we know about their contemporary status with particular emphasis on architecture, technology, customs, and celebrations. Each group is to provide information for a retrieval chart that Winston outlines.

When the students complete the chart, they recognize that the various tribes have similarities and many differences. They also recognize that their own thinking about American Indians has been limited. Even their vocabulary is affected by their research.

"We now realize that there is a difference between tribes, bands, and federations," said one student. "How would you like us to be different as a result of this study?" asks Winston. "Well," suggests a student, "we can make it a rule—well, I guess I mean a practice—that whenever possible we will refer to American Indians by specific tribal names. You know, like we'll say the Nez Perce or the Algonquin, like that." Another student chimes in, "I think we need to do this for everybody. We tend to do the same with Asians. We should differentiate between Chinese, Malaysians, Japanese, Vietnamese, and others."

This is just what Winston wants to hear. She asks the students to use the same techniques to develop a chart for Asians. She particularly seeks evidence of students' ability to distinguish similarities and differences before and after European contact and the Asian groups' contemporary status with particular emphasis on architecture, technology, customs, and celebrations, elements that students identified in their initial class discussion as likely areas of cross-cultural impact.

⊕ *Time, Continuity, & Change*

Social studies programs should include experiences that provide for the study of *the ways human beings view themselves in and over time*, so that the learner can:

Performance Expectations   **Related Themes**

a. demonstrate an understanding that different scholars may describe the same event or situation in different ways but must provide reasons or evidence for their views;   Ⅰ Ⅲ Ⅴ

b. identify and use key concepts such as chronology, causality, change, conflict, and complexity to explain, analyze, and show connections among patterns of historical change and continuity;   Ⅰ Ⅲ Ⅴ Ⅷ

c. identify and describe selected historical periods and patterns of change within and across cultures, such as the rise of civilizations, the development of transportation systems, the growth and breakdown of colonial systems, and others;   Ⅰ Ⅴ Ⅷ Ⅹ

d. identify and use processes important to reconstructing and reinterpreting the past, such as using a variety of sources, providing, validating, and weighing evidence for claims, checking credibility of sources, and searching for causality;   Ⅰ Ⅲ Ⅹ

e. develop critical sensitivities such as empathy and skepticism regarding attitudes, values, and behaviors of people in different historical contexts;   Ⅰ Ⅲ Ⅴ Ⅵ Ⅶ Ⅷ Ⅸ

f. use knowledge of facts and concepts drawn from history, along with methods of historical inquiry, to inform decision-making about and action-taking on public issues.   Ⅴ Ⅵ Ⅶ Ⅷ Ⅸ Ⅹ

FOCUS ON THE CLASSROOM: STANDARDS INTO PRACTICE

Example #1
Performance Expectations: b, c, d, e, f

Using the district basal reader for sixth grade, Cathryn Baerwald has her class engage in a study of the Middle Ages. The students are reading *Door in the Wall* and *Max and Me and the Time Machine*. As they read and discuss these books, they are simultaneously researching language, courtly manners, customs, and food, using library resources.

Baerwald decides that a unifying focus is needed to link the many aspects of life in the Middle Ages. She proposes that the students explore in depth a problem from this time period—one that involved personal decision-making about an ethical or moral dilemma. After she explains the basis of moral and ethical dilemmas to the students and explores with them dilemmas that all people face in their daily lives, the students review a list of problems involving individuals during the Middle Ages. Among the problems reviewed are those associated with Thomas à Becket and Joan of Arc, two individuals whose religious beliefs put them into conflict with the state. After Baerwald discusses the two stories with the students, they decide to concentrate on Thomas à Becket's conflict with the King of England, focusing on this question: "Should the priorities of government rule when they conflict with personal religious commitments?"

The students review the facts of the conflict and prepare a mock trial scenario under the direction of Baerwald. To accurately re-create the setting of the time period, students design and create clothing that simulates dress of the Middle Ages, and they ask the music and art teachers to help them decorate the classroom and provide music of the period using recordings and possibly guest vocalists or instrumentalists. Students develop roles for the mock trial based upon their understanding of English society in the Middle Ages, and then present the mock trial using a timed format adapted from national mock trial guidelines. The mock trial takes three class periods, and with the assistance of the school's audiovisual technician, it is videotaped.

After the mock trial has concluded, Baerwald and the students review excerpts from the videotape. She discusses with the students their reactions to the arguments presented in the trial, and has them evaluate the effectiveness of their efforts as a group against these criteria: use of historically accurate information, clarity of visual and spoken presentations, use of relevant examples, and the ability to maintain characterizations during the roleplay. As a means of assessing individual student learning, she has students write a reflective essay stating how they would have responded personally to the problem had they been Becket, and provide reasons for their response.

Example #2
Performance Expectations: a, b, c, d, e, f

Matt Laufer's eighth grade class has been studying the American Revolution by reading various accounts of the events leading up to the outbreak of war, including the textbook. In addition to these historical accounts, half the class has been assigned to read *Johnny Tremain* (a romanticized view of the American Revolution from the point of view of the Patriots), while the other half has read *My Brother Sam Is Dead* (which presents the perspectives of loyalists, rebels, pacifists, and undecided colonists).

After students complete the novels, Laufer assigns students to work in small groups, according to which book they read. Each group is to discuss the following questions:

1) According to each novel, what was the American Revolution like for ordinary people in colonial America?

2) What are the differences in the point of view of each author?

3) Based on these two stories, what conclusions might you draw about the dilemmas colonial Americans faced at the outbreak of war? What sources could you use to confirm your hypotheses?

4) Since one event may be portrayed in different ways, what might a citizen today do to get an accurate view of a contemporary issue?

Following their group discussion, each student hands in his or her own answers to the questions discussed by the group.

To assess their understanding of multiple perspectives, Laufer has his students work with partners or in small groups, gathering information about a contemporary issue from different perspectives. The students develop a list of criteria for assessing the information they gather, emphasizing credibility, detection of bias, accuracy of information, balance in points of view, and ways to prove the validity of claims and generalizations. Each student then prepares a news story and an editorial about the issue. After getting feedback and editorial assistance from their writing groups, each student prepares a final copy that Laufer uses for the final assessment. The criteria he uses for evaluation are: 1) the ability to list and apply at least three criteria for evaluating information, 2) providing credible evidence for claims made about events and conditions, and 3) providing reasonable and accurate support for the editorial position.

Example #3
Performance Expectations: a, b, d, e, f

Jamie Demarest's seventh grade class is studying slavery in the Western Hemisphere. On the chalkboard Demarest writes a question for investigation: "How can nations advocating the principles of equality, liberty, justice, and the essential dignity of all humans justify the institution of slavery?" Demarest was concerned that students would encounter a perspective on slavery that was narrowly defined if they used a limited range of sources. He therefore put together a resource packet for his students, including first-person accounts of slavery by ex-slaves, slaveholders, abolitionists, business people involved in the slave trade, maritime trade and cash crop production, and government officials. These packets included sources from the United States, Great Britain, Haiti, Africa, and France, all during the period 1700 through 1850.

All students have the same resource packet, but in order to facilitate a careful examination of all relevant perspectives on the question, Demarest assigns five groups in the class to represent different perspectives on the controversy: slaves, slaveholders, abolitionists, government officials, and business people. Each group prepares by reading all the resources in the packet, and responding to these questions: 1) What is the point of view of the source on the issue of slavery? 2) How does the author develop an argument pro or con? and 3) What are the implications for government policy of the author's argument? Having read all the resources in the total packet, the students then prepare a position paper that accurately represents the views of their assigned perspective, and attempts to rebut the arguments of groups who would oppose their position.

Demarest has each group present its position, after which the other groups can ask questions and provide rebuttal during a limited time frame. Demarest takes notes and develops a brief summary of the major points for review by the entire class. When he does so the next day, he asks students to check the accuracy of their positions as he summarized them. The students then discuss how their group positions relate to the ideals present in the investigation question. Demarest facilitates the exchange of views, emphasizing analysis of the relationship between stated ideals and actual policies.

At the conclusion of the full-class discussion, Demarest assigns the students to write an essay in which they will respond to the question for investigation by comparing their group's position to their own views on the topic. He also requires the students to critique the views of the other perspectives on the question before they search for a conclusion. Demarest evaluates the essays using the criteria of accuracy, impartiality, effective use of evidence, and logical development of argument.

 *People, Places, & Environments*

Social studies programs should include experiences that provide for the study of *people, places, and environments,* so that the learner can:

Performance Expectations   **Related Themes**

a. elaborate mental maps of locales, regions, and the world that demonstrate
understanding of relative location, direction, size, and shape;   **IX**

b. create, interpret, use, and distinguish various representations of the earth, such   **I** **II**
as maps, globes, and photographs;

c. use appropriate resources, data sources, and geographic tools such as aerial
photographs, satellite images, geographic information systems (GIS), map projections,
and cartography to generate, manipulate, and interpret information such as atlases,
data bases, grid systems, charts, graphs, and maps;

d. estimate distance, calculate scale, and distinguish other geographic relationships   **VIII** **IX**
such as population density and spatial distribution patterns;

e. locate and describe varying landforms and geographic features, such as mountains,   **VIII** **IX**
plateaus, islands, rain forests, deserts, and oceans, and explain their relationships
within the ecosystem;

f. describe physical system changes such as seasons, climate and weather, and the   **VIII** **IX**
water cycle and identify geographic patterns associated with them;

g. describe how people create places that reflect cultural values and ideals as they   **I** **II** **V** **VIII**
build neighborhoods, parks, shopping centers, and the like;

h. examine, interpret, and analyze physical and cultural patterns and their interactions,   **I** **II** **IX**
such as land use, settlement patterns, cultural transmission of customs and ideas,
and ecosystem changes;

i. describe ways that historical events have been influenced by, and have influenced,   **I** **II** **V** **VI**
physical and human geographic factors in local, regional, national, and global   **VII** **IX**
settings;

j. observe and speculate about social and economic effects of environmental changes   **V** **VII** **VIII**
and crises resulting from phenomena such as floods, storms, and drought;

k. propose, compare, and evaluate alternative uses of land and resources in   **V** **VII** **VIII** **IX**
communities, regions, nations, and the world.   **X**

FOCUS ON THE CLASSROOM: STANDARDS INTO PRACTICE

Example #1
Performance Expectations: b, c, e, h

Annie Gerner has her sixth grade class use globes to expand their understanding of the idea of human migration. During this activity, she divides the class into groups representing each continent. Each group researches its continent to identify cultural minority groups that have dwelt on the continent. Gerner then has individual students from each group select one of the minority cultures identified and trace its migration patterns over time. Each group creates a large map of its continent on which students illustrate the various cultures' migration patterns in a manner that is clear and easy to understand. Each group presents its findings to the class.

Gerner assesses each group presentation on its historical and geographic accuracy and the quality of the map. Each presentation is used to determine whether students are acquiring knowledge about human movement patterns and developing both research skills and the ability to communicate and present data and ideas.

Example #2
Performance Expectations: c, g, h

A unit within the world culture section of Sara Vertinen's seventh grade core class involves setting up a World Bank. The students have completed a unit on economic and social development of nations and regions and have begun to build an understanding of that broad concept. They know that a variety of factors can interact to support or constrain the economic and social development of an area. They are beginning to acquire an understanding of global interdependence and the ways in which supranational structures can support the development of particular areas.

In this new unit, some students, as bank officials, interview other students who represent selected nations in the developing world who are applying for loans to build infrastructure. Prior to these interviews, the students have gathered information about the climate, natural resources, potential labor forces, technical training facilities, and ability to repay the loan of the countries they represent. The location of each nation represented is plotted on the world map. Following the interviews, the World Bank "officials" gather together to decide which countries will receive loans and why.

Vertinen evaluates students on their ability to gather and interpret information from a variety of resources including maps and atlases. She will also assess their ability to compare and evaluate alternative land uses in particular nations. Their final proposal is to reflect this information and analysis.

Example #3
Performance Expectations: c, f, g, j, k

Bill Jones's eighth grade class has been involved in an interdisciplinary unit examining how the natural environment affects people and their lives. On this day, Jones tells his class that a natural disaster is eminent in the form of a hurricane that is predicted to hit their community. Students form groups of four each to take the role of a Civil Emergency Coordinating Committee. Their task is to speculate about the social and economic effects of the disaster and to determine mechanisms for coping with those effects. Among the decisions they must make is how much power to give to the government and how much to leave to the individual.

The students make a plan to guide the municipality through 48 hours, based on their inferences about social and economic needs. They examine the tension between

Middle Grades	individual rights and the needs of the group in making decisions about how to meet the disaster. At the end of the discussion, they make announcements for the local cable station and radio station and for broadsides to be distributed by emergency personnel.

Jones will assess each essay on the logic and clarity of the connection between the student's proposal and the possible social and economic consequences of the disaster. In addition, each essay must demonstrate that the student has considered both the good of the community and the individual rights of its residents.

Ⓘⓥ *Individual Development & Identity*

Social studies programs should include experiences that provide for the study of *individual development and identity*, so that the learner can:

Performance Expectations	Related Themes
a. relate personal changes to social, cultural, and historical contexts;	Ⓘ ⒾⒾ Ⓘⓧ
b. describe personal connections to place—as associated with community, nation, and world;	Ⓘ Ⓘ Ⓘ
c. describe the ways family, gender, ethnicity, nationality, and institutional affiliations contribute to personal identity;	Ⓘ Ⓥ
d. relate such factors as physical endowment and capabilities, learning, motivation, personality, perception, and behavior to individual development;	
e. identify and describe ways regional, ethnic, and national cultures influence individuals' daily lives;	Ⓘ Ⓘⓘ Ⓘⓘⓘ
f. identify and describe the influence of perception, attitudes, values, and beliefs on personal identity;	Ⓘ Ⓥ
g. identify and interpret examples of stereotyping, conformity, and altruism;	Ⓘ Ⓥ
h. work independently and cooperatively to accomplish goals.	Ⓧ

FOCUS ON THE CLASSROOM: STANDARDS INTO PRACTICE

Example #1
Performance Expectations: a, b, d, e, f, h

"The school theme for this year is 'You Can Make a Difference,'" Vicki Katz tells her sixth grade class. "We are going to look at how other people have made a difference." She writes on the board, "Ordinary people are capable of doing extraordinary things."

She then reads *Uncle Willy and the Soup Kitchen* to the children. The class discusses how Uncle Willy was a regular person, that there was a need to help hungry people, and he volunteered at the soup kitchen and enjoyed it.

Katz begins to construct a chart with the students:

What was happening in the community, state, nation, world?

What were some influences on the person?

What was the action of the person?

What were the results for others?

What were the results for the person?

Katz is pleased when several students bring in newspaper articles about this topic the next day. They add these stories to the chart. She gives a book talk on *Number the Stars, Snow Treasure, Sadako and the Thousand Paper Cranes,* and *Ahuoka and the Talking Leaves.* Each book is about extraordinary acts of ordinary people. Katz expects each person to read two or more of these books. She has ten copies of each title, sets aside classroom time to read, and allows students to take the books home for additional reading time. She also gives students a list of suggested readings from which they can select at least one more book to read.

When a parent calls Katz to tell her about a traveling exhibition called "Remember the Children," circulated by the United States Holocaust Memorial Council, she organizes a field trip to the exhibit. While there, the students notice many examples of extraordinary acts of courage on the part of ordinary people. Katz purchases several copies of *Daniel's Story* for the students to read. They have many items to fill in their chart when they return to school.

With this background, Katz introduces a personal chart for each person to record how he or she can make a difference. One student's reaction is "But I'm no hero." The other students reply, "Ordinary people can do extraordinary things!"

In order to assess achievement, Katz asks each child to apply the questions from the chart to one of the books she or he has read. Katz reviews their work for accuracy and clarity.

Example #2
Performance Expectations: d, f, h

Jim Samples has been working with his seventh grade class on the importance of careful decision-making and the various factors that influence individuals' decisions. He asks students to select a recent choice of some importance to them, but one that is not too personal for public discussion and for reflection and analysis of factors they considered in reaching a decision. As examples, he suggests decisions to try out for honor band or athletic team, not go to summer camp, or to join a club. As a class, the students share the decision-making factors they came up with; these included wants and needs, talents, interests, and influence of family members, peers, or media.

Each student, thinking of his or her own decision, charts the decision-making factors, sorting the various factors into pros and cons. Then each student assigns a weight to each influence. A weight of +3 is strongly positive; a weight of -3 is strongly negative. Each student discusses his or her choices, shows how the decision was reached, and explains what influences affected the decision and how each influence was weighted.

Clarity of the description of the choice, pro/con analysis with justifications for each weighing, the degree to which conclusions are supported by the student, and the quality of the student's presentation serve as criteria for evaluation.

Example #3
Performance Expectations: a, b, h

Henry Alston's eighth grade class has completed a two-week unit on the topics of how history is written and how it represents historians' interpretations of important events.

As the third week begins, Alston starts the class by saying, "History is someone's retelling of the past. Often the historian was not actually present at the event being described. Each of us has a personal history. Think back and select three or four events from your own past—events that form your own personal history. You have one advantage over most historians: you were personally present at the important events you select. You are going to become the author of a personal history. As a historian, you can leave out the details about each event that aren't important from your point of view and emphasize the parts that you select as important for us to know. You cannot deliberately make up any event in your personal history and should report each event as accurately as you can. Integrate your personal events with a few larger historical events that happened about the same time as your important personal events—for example, a presidential election or the beginning of the Gulf War. Write your history in a narrative form. Eventually, we will put your historical events on a poster in the form of a timeline and give the timeline a title such as 'The Life and Times of Jennifer Northcross.'"

The students begin writing. They select important national and/or international events that have occurred during their lifetimes and recall important events in their own lives. In the last fifteen minutes of the class, Alston asks the students to meet in groups of three to read their life histories to each other. He asks them to choose one member of the group who will read his or her history to the class tomorrow.

The next day nine students read their histories. The students are amazed at how interesting their classmates' lives have been in thirteen short years. Some have moved many times and have lived in various parts of the country; some have traveled to unique places; and some have endured illnesses and other challenges. The students also notice that they often selected national and international events that were linked to their own lives. For example, James selected the Persian Gulf War because an uncle served in the army during the war; and Marge selected the launch of a space shuttle from Cape Canaveral because she was living near there at the time.

Next, the students each construct a timeline, finding or drawing pictures and photos to illustrate their histories. Alston gives the following instructions: "Select one of the national or international events you remember best, and write a three-paragraph essay that includes: one paragraph that describes what you remember as important about the event, one paragraph after you read two or more historical accounts of the event, and a third paragraph explaining how the historical accounts differ and why you believe the differences exist."

Alston uses this activity as a springboard to have students examine the role of historians in the writing of history. He has the students reflect on the differences between their memory of events and the accounts by historians, considering such questions as why some accounts are more detailed than others, why historians include different facts, and why two or more historians consulted about the same event sometimes disagree with each other. Alston knows that one way for his students to appreciate history as a reconstruction of the past is to try to write history for themselves. He also knows that the students will discover that what is reported as history is selected by each historian, often because of what is significant to that historian, and that students will recognize the need to explore the many voices of history that give life to any specific historical event or period. Alston reads each essay to determine the plan of the essay and to assess the logic of the reasons cited for differences between historical accounts.

Ⓥ *Individuals, Groups, & Institutions*

Social studies programs should include experiences that provide for the study of *interactions among individuals, groups, and institutions,* so that the learner can:

Performance Expectations   **Related Themes**

a. demonstrate an understanding of concepts such as role, status, and social class in describing the interactions of individuals and social groups;   **I** **IV**

b. analyze group and institutional influences on people, events, and elements of culture;   **I** **II** **IV** **VI** **X**

c. describe the various forms institutions take and the interactions of people with institutions;   **I** **VI** **X**

d. identify and analyze examples of tensions between expressions of individuality and group or institutional efforts to promote social conformity;   **I** **II** **IV** **VI** **X**

e. identify and describe examples of tensions between belief systems and government policies and laws;   **I** **II** **IV** **VI** **X**

f. describe the role of institutions in furthering both continuity and change;   **I** **II** **VI** **VIII** **X**

g. apply knowledge of how groups and institutions work to meet individual needs and promote the common good.   **I** **II** **VI** **X**

FOCUS ON THE CLASSROOM: STANDARDS INTO PRACTICE

Example #1
Performance Expectations: a, b, f

Maria Foseide's sixth grade students have been examining current events with respect to the role various institutions (e.g., religious, social, and political) play in the decisions and actions of individuals, groups, and nations. Students have come to recognize the interrelationships between events and the institutions that shape them.

Having familiarized her students with political cartoons through frequent use of them during the year, Foseide has the students create cartoons that reflect the role of one or more institutions in a selected event. Ability to accurately identify the role of the institution(s) in the event and clarity and quality of presentation in cartoon format serve as criteria for evaluating evidence of understanding.

Example #2
Performance Expectations: b, c, d, e, f

Nick Grafton has his seventh grade geography students research the history and purposes of the Ku Klux Klan. With the assistance of the school's librarian, Grafton has them find articles related to recent Klan activities and locate these on a map of the United States. After completing their maps, the students, working in groups, examine whether geographic patterns of activity emerge and predict whether this activity will or will not affect race relations in these areas.

Grafton and the students select five communities for further study. The selection is based on a cross-section of community size and includes communities where Grafton knows another teacher through professional associations, summer institutes, and other meetings. Grafton contacts the other teachers and asks them to assist in the project by identifying newspapers and libraries in their area; he also asks about their willingness to respond to student inquiries. Students form groups, and each group writes to the library in one of the five communities, asking for reprints from the local newspaper of any articles about Klan activities. They also prepare and send a brief list of questions about the activities to Grafton's teacher friends; these questions are prepared on the basis of the articles they receive and the stories reported nationally on wire services. The students in Grafton's class look forward to the mail's arrival daily and keep a journal of the clippings and responses they receive.

At the end of the six weeks, the students review and analyze their findings. Their first objective is to analyze the degree to which local reports and those from national publications present the same information about any events reported in both and, where differences occur, consider why they might exist. Their second charge is to test their predictions and examine the effects of the Klan on the communities observed. Each group presents its findings to the class, using the strategies of investigative reporting.

The effectiveness of presentations, reporting accuracy, and use of adequate documentation serve as criteria for Grafton to evaluate each group's work.

Example #3
Performance Expectations: c, d, f, g

Dorothy McDonald's eighth grade students are studying the pre-Civil War era. Although the students seem to be able to remember the facts of the era, they do not seem to have a sense of the interplay of individuals, groups, and institutions in bringing about societal change. McDonald decides to raise the following questions with her students: "Can individuals change society? Can groups? Can institutions?" She divides the students into three groups, one each for individuals, groups, and institutions to investigate the question. She tells students they can answer the question any way they want, except for giving a written report. Most students are relieved to know they don't have to write a paper. However, they soon learn that they may be doing even more work to answer the question by not using the familiar format of a written report.

McDonald suggests some examples for investigation. They include Frederick Douglass, John Brown, the Grimké sisters, Harriet Beecher Stowe, representatives at the Seneca Falls Convention, state and federal courts (including the Supreme Court), Abraham Lincoln/the Presidency, and leaders of Congress. Students suggest more possibilities.

Over the next week, students research and talk with each other about how they will make their case. McDonald focuses the class on leaders of the abolitionist movement as a case study for understanding reform. At the end of the week, the three groups make presentations that support their notions about how individuals, groups, and institutions could change society. One group does a magazine exposé of the terrible conditions endured by slaves in the South. A second group does a panel presentation fea-

Middle Grades

turing well-known individuals from the era who explain how they thought their work would make a better society. The third group convenes a meeting of people who were working for suffrage rights for women and African-Americans.

The overwhelming conclusion of the class is that all three—individuals, groups, and institutions—can and do make changes in the society. As a followup, McDonald asks students to develop a list in each category of present-day people who are working for social change. McDonald assesses the quality of the group projects by determining how effectively they use accurate historical information, the degree to which they evaluate the strengths and weaknesses of reform efforts, and the clarity and logical development of the arguments used to reach conclusions.

VI *Power, Authority, & Governance*

Social studies programs should include experiences that provide for the study of *how people create and change structures of power, authority, and governance*, so that the learner can:

Performance Expectations   **Related Themes**

a. examine persistent issues involving the rights, roles, and status of the individual in relation to the general welfare;   **II V X**

b. describe the purpose of government and how its powers are acquired, used, and justified;   **X**

c. analyze and explain ideas and governmental mechanisms to meet needs and wants of citizens, regulate territory, manage conflict, and establish order and security;   **I V IX**

d. describe the ways nations and organizations respond to forces of unity and diversity affecting order and security;   **I II V**

e. identify and describe the basic features of the political system in the United States, and identify representative leaders from various levels and branches of government;   **X**

f. explain conditions, actions, and motivations that contribute to conflict and cooperation within and among nations;   **II IX**

g. describe and analyze the role of technology in communications, transportation, information-processing, weapons development, or other areas as it contributes to or helps resolve conflicts;   **VII VIII IX**

h. explain and apply concepts such as power, role, status, justice, and influence to the examination of persistent issues and social problems;   **I II V**

i. give examples and explain how governments attempt to achieve their stated ideals at home and abroad.   **IX X**

FOCUS ON THE CLASSROOM: STANDARDS INTO PRACTICE

Example #1
Performance Expectations: a, b

Students in Juliet Singer's eighth grade social studies class have just been told that their school will no longer offer music instruction because the Board of Education had to cut $25,000 from the budget. Singer's class has been studying communities and community/school governance, and the students want to know how and why such a change in their program could happen. Singer asks a member of the school board to speak to the class about the music decision.

After the class has met with the school board member and held discussions about the school budget, Singer asks the class if they can think of a way to save the music program by cutting something else in the budget or by raising more money from the community or a combination of both. Small groups of students research how the costs of music programs compare to other programs, such as reading, science, and sports. Other groups explore the possibilities of raising taxes. Others investigate community support for music.

After the groups come together and discuss their findings, they prepare a statement for the school board on what they think the board should do, including PTA and student fundraising activities. Singer and the students evaluate the students' policy statement for clarity of the recommended policy, accuracy and completeness of the data used to support the recommendation, and evidence of consideration of conflicting views.

When the students have refined their policy recommendation, they send it to the board. After the board receives the recommendation, students appoint a committee to speak on behalf of their plan at the school board meeting. Singer invites a board member to speak to the class again and explain how the process of change will move forward if their plan is accepted.

Example #2
Performance Expectations: b, c, d, f, h, i

John Crawford's fifth grade class is nearing the end of a unit on how governments have used their power to maintain order and stability. They have already read a case study of how the British tried to control the American colonists prior to the Revolutionary War and have viewed videotapes showing how the Soviet Union dealt with the Baltic Republics when they attempted to break away and declare their independence. During their discussions, the students develop a chart listing different ways that governments responded in such situations and which specific governing philosophies are most consistent with the various choices.

To help students see how these various choices led to quite different results, Crawford introduces a computer simulation on revolutions. The simulation involves a hypothetical state threatening to break away from its republic. Crawford organizes the students into teams after helping them set their priorities among several choices for action. As teams choose their alternatives, their next set of choices is determined. Teams debate their various options before each move, and on each team a team historian records the possible choices and the reasoning behind each move in the simulation as well as the random events generated by the computer. At the conclusion of the simulation, teams compare their scores, based on how well they achieved their original objectives. Then the class discusses what they learned about the results of employing power in different ways and how making different choices really did lead to different results. As the period ends, Sharon observes that if the British had responded differently to the demands of the colonists, we might not have to study United States history in the eleventh grade.

For homework, Crawford poses a series of historical and contemporary situations in which a specific government's decisions produced certain results. He includes the American Revolution, the Bolshevik Revolution of 1917, the Soviet-Baltic conflict, and the conflict in Northern Ireland. Each student compares his or her findings from the simulation to the four situations and suggests how alternative government policies may have resulted in different outcomes. Crawford evaluates the written responses recorded in the team historian's log on the basis of clear and cogent reasoning, establishment of direct linkages between causes and proposed effects, and analysis of the relationship between government philosophies and policy choices.

Ⅶ *Production, Distribution, & Consumption*

Social studies programs should include experiences that provide for the study of *how people organize for the production, distribution, and consumption of goods and services,* so that the learner can:

Performance Expectations	Related Themes
a. give and explain examples of ways that economic systems structure choices about how goods and services are to be produced and distributed;	I III VI
b. describe the role that supply and demand, prices, incentives, and profits play in determining what is produced and distributed in a competitive market system;	V VI IX
c. explain the difference between private and public goods and services;	V VI
d. describe a range of examples of the various institutions that make up economic systems such as households, business firms, banks, government agencies, labor unions, and corporations;	V IX
e. describe the role of specialization and exchange in the economic process;	V VIII IX
f. explain and illustrate how values and beliefs influence different economic decisions;	I IX
g. differentiate among various forms of exchange and money;	I IX
h. compare basic economic systems according to who determines what is produced, distributed, and consumed;	I V VI IX
i. use economic concepts to help explain historical and current developments and issues in local, national, or global contexts;	I II IX
j. use economic reasoning to compare different proposals for dealing with a contemporary social issue such as unemployment, acid rain, or high quality education.	V VI VIII IX X

FOCUS ON THE CLASSROOM: STANDARDS INTO PRACTICE

Example #1
Performance Expectations: c, d, f, i, j

A city is trying to decide whether to develop a property as a park or to allow a developer to build a strip mall and condos. Paul Fraser's fifth grade class has been following events related to the property since the decision was made to tear down the current structure. The class has been studying economic decision-making with emphasis on the economic reasons behind decisions.

Fraser divides the class into a park group and a developer group, each of which researches the pros and cons of both sides in order to persuade the city council to adopt their plan. Larry Stricklin, principal, Beth Schultz, teacher of Environmental Studies at the high school, and Arlene Cornwall, owner of a local company, come in to hear the deliberations. They are given the same set of criteria the groups were given to make a decision. They find merit in the developer groups' presentation stressing short-term benefits of building a strip mall and condos, and compliment the group on its charts showing possible income from the proposed development. However, they decide the park group offered a more compelling case. In the long run, they reason, the city will attract other businesses and families that will financially support the city.

Although the students in the developer group are disappointed, they feel they presented a good case. The park group students are, of course, delighted with the decision.

The next day Fraser leads a debriefing session, discussing how both cases could have been strengthened, given the comments of the three visiting panelists.

Example #2
Performance Expectations: a, e, f, h, i

Patti Barbes's sixth graders use the newspaper as a primary text for their work in social studies, language arts, science, and health. Recent articles have stressed problems related to the availability of adequate food supplies in parts of Africa, in economically distressed regions of the United States, and in the local community.

Barbes recognizes that her students do not have an understanding of the problems associated with making decisions dealing with distribution of limited food supplies. She divides the class into six working groups and gives each group an apple. Each group must decide who will get the apple. There are initial shouts of "Me! Me! Me!" In one group, the first person to grab the apple refuses to give it up. These initial reactions give way to intense discussions about dividing the apples. A coin toss is proposed, and one group tries to determine who has the greatest need.

After each group shares its solutions and its difficulties in coming to a conclusion, Barbes asks each student to consider how the group's deliberations might have been different if they all were experiencing a very limited and inadequate diet. After students write their reactions in their journals, Barbes leads a discussion of their reactions.

This activity is used as a reference point in discussions of related news stories in the weeks ahead. Some students elect to do volunteer work at a local food distribution center, sharing their experiences and observations with the class.

Example #3
Performance Expectations: b, d, e, f, h, i

John Van Horn's eighth grade history class is studying the Civil War. One of the goals for the unit is to develop an understanding of the way in which the pre-war economy was disrupted by the war.

Van Horn divides the class into study groups. One group explores a variety of sources dealing with the impact of the war on economic activity in the Northeast. Another group studies the impact of the war on the cotton plantation South. The wartime economy of the Northwest is explored by still another group, while other students examine the war's effect on farming and ranching in the Southwest. In addition, they consider aspects of international trade and wartime blockades, as well as wartime disruptions of established transportation systems.

Van Horn works with each group to focus its study on the impact of political division and conflict on the sectional economies throughout the United States. Each group makes a series of reports using a variety of formats, including a video newscast, maps, graphs, Hypercard™ stacks, and a news magazine. Van Horn assesses the quality of the projects on the basis of selections of appropriate themes, accuracy of supporting information, specified relationships of sectional interests to national issues, and international dimensions of sectional economic developments, as well as the clarity and organization of the presentations.

Middle Grades

Ⅷ *Science, Technology, & Society*

Social studies programs should include experiences that provide for the study of *relationships among science, technology, and society,* so that the learner can:

Performance Expectations   **Related Themes**

a. examine and describe the influence of culture on scientific and technological choices and advancement, such as in transportation, medicine, and warfare;

Ⅰ Ⅱ Ⅴ Ⅸ

b. show through specific examples how science and technology have changed people's perceptions of the social and natural world, such as in their relationship to the land, animal life, family life, and economic needs, wants, and security;

Ⅰ Ⅱ Ⅲ Ⅴ
Ⅵ Ⅶ Ⅸ

c. describe examples in which values, beliefs, and attitudes have been influenced by new scientific and technological knowledge, such as the invention of the printing press, conceptions of the universe, applications of atomic energy, and genetic discoveries;

Ⅰ Ⅱ Ⅲ Ⅴ
Ⅸ Ⅹ

d. explain the need for laws and policies to govern scientific and technological applications, such as in the safety and well-being of workers and consumers and the regulation of utilities, radio, and television;

Ⅵ Ⅶ Ⅸ Ⅹ

e. seek reasonable and ethical solutions to problems that arise when scientific advancements and social norms or values come into conflict.

Ⅰ Ⅴ Ⅵ Ⅹ

FOCUS ON THE CLASSROOM: STANDARDS INTO PRACTICE

Focus #1
Performance Expectations: a, b, c

Each week during part of their class, Carol Binford's seventh graders play "If it hadn't been for" as they examine a current event. They volunteer statements that begin with "If it hadn't been for" that enumerate and explain factors that caused or came to bear on the event. Binford asks students not only to list human choices and events that led to the event under study, but also scientific and technological knowledge and innovations that enabled the event to come to pass.

From time to time, Binford asks a student or small group to complete an "If it hadn't been for" mural to trace the complexity of factors leading to an event of particular interest or impact. Students develop charts, pictures, and other graphics to illustrate the chain of events. This "webbing" of causality provides an excellent visual reminder that only rarely is a single factor responsible for an event and that technology increasingly plays a major role in contemporary events.

Twice during the semester, Binford asks students to write a one- or two-page paper about an event she describes for them. She is careful to select an event they have not used already in their "If it hadn't been for" exercises. In their essays, they are to enumerate and explain how scientific and technological knowledge and innovations are related to the event. She evaluates each essay on the basis of accuracy and completeness of analysis, clarity of presentation, and grammar and spelling.

Example #2

Performance Expectations: b, c

Lynn Fuller-Bailie's sixth graders are computer game junkies who are not the least bit intimidated by computers, laserdiscs, or interactive video. They take the world of computer technology for granted. In fact, they can't believe how ancient societies and cultures existed without the modern conveniences they have grown to love and need. Fuller-Bailie wants them to understand that science and technology are not just the province of the late twentieth century.

Fuller-Bailie borrows some art prints of the Seven Wonders of the World from Alice Walters, the art teacher. Walters knows how to make slides from the prints and agrees to work with Fuller-Bailie on this project. Walters makes two sets of slides of each of the Seven Wonders: the Temple of Artemis, the Statue of Zeus, the Pyramids of Egypt, the Lighthouse at Alexandria, the Hanging Gardens of Babylon, the Mausoleum of Halicarnassus, and the Colossus of Rhodes. The students in Fuller-Bailie's class are charged with finding out what technologies permitted the people to build these architectural wonders and how these technologies challenged and changed the environment. Fuller-Bailie wants the students to re-evaluate the Seven Wonders in relation to subsequent structures. She begins collecting photos and pictures of Frank Lloyd Wright buildings, the Golden Gate Bridge, the Sears Tower, the Eiffel Tower, the TransAmerican Pyramid, the Tokyo Cathedral, a geodesic dome, the Great Wall of China, and the Washington Monument. Students are to come up with a revised list of Seven Wonders and justify the replacement of any of the original wonders.

In Walters's art class, the students build replicas of the seven wonders and design a structure of their own that is worth being called an Eighth Wonder. They describe the technology necessary to build their wonder and consider the costs and benefits to society. Walters evaluates each student's project on its creativity and aesthetic qualities. Fuller-Bailie evaluates the written part of the assignment using three criteria: analysis of the relationship between technology and building structure, the description of the potential impact of those technologies on the environment, and clarity of writing, including the use of correct grammar and spelling.

Example #3

Performance Expectations: a, d, e

Eighth graders in Tom Gwin's class have been studying the Eight Amendment to the U.S. Constitution. They have discussed the clauses and developed a good understanding of each of the parts. In discussing the clause "nor cruel and inhuman punishments inflicted," they consider whether the death penalty should be allowed. The class splits on the issue because some members of the class feel some forms of capital punishment such as electrocution and hanging are "cruel," others because they feel it is immoral, and still others because it does not work to deter violent crimes. When they come into class on Wednesday, Gwin poses the following statement, "Death by lethal injection as a form of capital punishment should be allowed in the United States." After clarifying the meaning of "lethal" and what death by lethal injection entails, Gwin begins a discussion of the issue with the question "What are various points of view on this issue?"

Kim answers, "Who is to carry out the sentence? A doctor? It is a violation of the Hippocratic oath to ask a physician to cause someone's death. It doesn't matter if a jury has said that the convicted criminal should die. It's wrong."

Hans comes back with, "Wait a minute. The death penalty is the death penalty. It doesn't matter how someone is executed. This way is cheap and more humane than hanging or electrocution."

Gwin asks Kim to stand on the far left of the front of the room and Hans on the far right. Then he asks Emily where she stands on the issue. Emily responds: "I think that sometimes people should be executed. If they had a fair trial and the jury found them guilty, they should die." Emily assumes a position midway between Kim and Hans. Other students join in the conversation, taking an appropriate place on the continuum. As those who have already taken a stand listen to their classmates talk, they sometimes move toward one end or the other of the continuum.

That night, students explain in their journals their position on the issue and reasons for it. They mention the arguments their classmates had given which did or did not influence them to change their own position.

The following day, Gwin shows students a videotape in which several experts debate the morality and legality of capital punishment and the use of various ways to implement it. Students also use their classroom computer to search a data base for answers to questions such as: How many people were executed in each state over the last ten years? What is the correlation between the crime rate in a state and the number of criminals who are put to death each year? How many other countries use capital punishment and what are their crime rates? The class then suggests how these data can best be presented in tables and charts, and various groups then transfer the data into such forms. Another group abstracts the different arguments presented in the videotape.

The next day, Gwin divides the class into teams of five and asks them to prepare reports on the following topics: facts and generalizations about capital punishment; arguments for and against the use of the death sentence as a form of punishment; arguments for and against capital punishment as a deterrent to violent crime; views on various forms of capital punishment; alternatives to capital punishment; and predictions of what would happen if capital punishment were abolished.

As a final assignment, Gwin asks each student to write a brief essay stating his or her position on capital punishment and indicating what he or she believes would be the ideal policy on capital punishment. Students must support their positions with data and arguments discussed during the unit. Gwin evaluates their papers using the following criteria: clarity of argument, use of data to support the argument, and quality of writing, including spelling and grammar.

Ⓘ *Global Connections*

Social studies programs should include experiences that provide for the study of *global connections and interdependence*, so that the learner can:

Performance Expectations	Related Themes
a. describe instances in which language, art, music, belief systems, and other cultural elements can facilitate global understanding or cause misunderstanding;	Ⓘ Ⓘ Ⓘ
b. analyze examples of conflict, cooperation, and interdependence among groups, societies, and nations;	Ⓥ Ⓥ
c. describe and analyze the effects of changing technologies on the global community;	Ⓥ
d. explore the causes, consequences, and possible solutions to persistent, contemporary, and emerging global issues, such as health, security, resource allocation, economic development, and environmental quality;	Ⓘ Ⓥ
e. describe and explain the relationships and tensions between national sovereignty and global interests in such matters as territory, natural resources, trade, use of technology, and welfare of people;	Ⓥ Ⓥ Ⓥ
f. demonstrate understanding of concerns, standards, issues, and conflicts related to universal human rights;	Ⓥ Ⓧ
g. identify and describe the roles of international and multinational organizations.	Ⓥ Ⓥ

FOCUS ON THE CLASSROOM: STANDARDS INTO PRACTICE

Example #1
Performance Expectations: b, d, g

Margi Rodriguez prepares a list of businesses and organizations in the city, trying to include as many as possible of those who have been involved in education or supported the school system in the past. She and her seventh grade social studies students construct a brief survey to identify ways in which these businesses and organizations have global connections. Students each select one of the businesses or organizations to contact and survey. Rodriguez assists students in developing the necessary confidence to approach the proper individuals to request time from their busy schedules for an interview.

With the exception of a few predictable rough spots, students are successful in completing their surveys. They then compile their findings and discover both expected and unexpected patterns regarding the global connections that exist in the local business community. They find that some companies have foreign workers, use equipment or parts originating outside the United States, have parent or satellite companies in other countries, or export their products or services to other countries. Each student develops a poster or graphic that illustrates either the information gathered by that student or a compilation of the findings of the class. To accompany the graphic, each student also prepares a brief statement in the form of a news story, which is videotaped and shared with the company each student contacted. Accuracy and quality of presentation, thoroughness of effort to identify ways in which the assigned company has global connections, and analysis of data serve as criteria to evaluate evidence of understanding.

Example #2

Performance Expectations: a, b

At the beginning of the school year, Paula King has her sixth graders brainstorm a lengthy list of topics they wish to know about upon completion of units on each region of the world. By consensus, a final list of approximately 25 topics is agreed upon, including some that are predictable, such as what kind of sports and games are popular in each region, and others that are less predictable, such as what kinds of natural disasters are most common in each region. King encourages the inclusion of additional topics, such as quality of life indicators of nations within the regions and the social, economic, and cultural needs of their people.

As each unit is begun, students in cooperative learning groups randomly draw a number of the topics for which they become responsible. As they begin a new region, each group will address new topics, so that over the course of the year, most students experience exploring most topics. At times, new topics are added, and on occasion, a topic is deemed either relatively unimportant or too difficult to research and is deleted. Student groups may choose either to divide the topics and work independently, or work collectively on each, one at a time. Most try one method one time and the other another time, finding that neither is perfect. No matter the strategy, the need for joint effort and commitment quickly becomes apparent, and the tremendous influence of peer pressure in this age group invariably comes to bear.

King supports each group's efforts, providing resources and ideas for ways to access elusive information. At the conclusion of each unit, students prepare class presentations that often include a number of data sources, including maps, charts, and tables. Effectiveness, accuracy, and clarity of the presentations, student-generated group effectiveness evaluations, and self-evaluations form the basis of teacher assessment.

Example #3

Performance Expectations: a, e, f

The eighth-grade students in Michael Reggio's classes are arguing about the 1991 war in the Persian Gulf. Some of the students feel that the United States should have stayed longer and inflicted more damage on Iraq to ensure that Saddam Hussein could not regain military and political power. Other students feel that the United States had no business in the Persian Gulf in the first place, citing domestic problems as a more important place to focus U.S. efforts and resources. As the groups argue back and forth, it becomes apparent to Reggio that neither has an understanding of the cultures of the people who inhabit the Persian Gulf region. The students speak in stereotypes and generalizations about Arab peoples and the religion of Islam. Reggio decides to address the problem. He contacts the international center at a nearby university and arranges for students from several Islamic cultures to come and meet with his class. He asks the university students to spend some time focusing on the basic tenets of Islam and the importance of the religion to their culture.

This experience created a model for future units. Now, as each new region of the world is introduced, Reggio has students generate a description of how they view countries and cultures of the region based upon their limited information. By consulting international visitors provided by the university and resources suggested by them for further study, students' stereotypes and misunderstandings are examined. To culminate a year of combatting stereotyping and increasing cultural sensitivity, Reggio has his students examine a series of letters to the editor he has collected over the years that in one way or another reflect a lack of respect or sensitivity to groups of specific cultures, genders, races, physical characteristics or abilities, or special interests. He has students respond to these letters as if they were members of the group. He uses the writing process to help students produce publishable letters. These are then shared and evaluated in terms of clarity of purpose, accuracy of information, form, and effectiveness of presentation.

ⓧ *Civic Ideals & Practices*

Social studies programs should include experiences that provide for the study of *the ideals, principles, and practices of citizenship in a democratic republic*, so that the learner can:

Performance Expectations   **Related Themes**

a. examine the origins and continuing influence of key ideals of the democratic republican   **Ⅱ Ⅴ Ⅵ**
form of government, such as individual human dignity, liberty, justice, equality, and the rule
of law;

b. identify and interpret sources and examples of the rights and responsibilities of citizens;   **Ⅱ**

c. locate, access, analyze, organize, and apply information about selected public issues—   **Ⅰ Ⅱ Ⅴ Ⅸ**
recognizing and explaining multiple points of view;

d. practice forms of civic discussion and participation consistent with the ideals of citizens   **Ⅱ Ⅴ Ⅵ**
in a democratic republic;

e. explain and analyze various forms of citizen action that influence public policy decisions;   **Ⅰ Ⅴ Ⅵ**

f. identify and explain the roles of formal and informal political actors in influencing and   **Ⅴ Ⅵ**
shaping public policy and decision-making;

g. analyze the influence of diverse forms of public opinion on the development of public   **Ⅴ Ⅵ**
policy and decision-making;

h. analyze the effectiveness of selected public policies and citizen behaviors in realizing the   **Ⅱ Ⅴ Ⅵ Ⅸ**
stated ideals of a democratic republican form of government;

i. explain the relationship between policy statements and action plans used to address issues   **Ⅵ**
of public concern;

j. examine strategies designed to strengthen the "common good," which consider a range   **Ⅱ Ⅴ Ⅵ**
of options for citizen action.

FOCUS ON THE CLASSROOM: STANDARDS INTO PRACTICE

Example #1
Performance Expectations: c, d, e, f, h, i, j

Following an incident in which a student at a local high school threatened another student with a handgun, Janet Morton's fifth graders begin collecting news reports about other incidents in schools involving weapons. Morton invites an attorney specializing in youth offenses to visit her classroom to respond to questions the students have raised regarding laws governing minors and weapon possession and use. They learn that there is no law currently on the books specifically prohibiting youth from carrying handguns, in or out of school. As a result, the school system's only recourse has been to establish a policy stating that any student possessing a deadly weapon will be immediately suspended and automatically face an expulsion hearing. This measure, in the attorney's opinion, is an insufficient response to the growing problem of weapons in schools. The students agree and, with the attorney's voluntary assistance, create a plan to lobby their state legislature for tougher laws governing minors and weapons. Morton's job is to help them understand the process of enacting law.

The class begins by charting the progress of an idea from simply being a stated need to becoming a law. They then conduct research, with the help of their attorney mentor, to discover what laws currently exist governing the possession and use of weapons. They examine the wording and construction of a bill and prepare a draft to present before their school Parent Teacher Association (PTA) board in hopes of garnering their support and possible partnership in their effort to strengthen existing law. The PTA board members agree and join the students in going before the school board, again to try and win their support. Again they are successful, even though one member has to be persuaded by the social studies supervisor that Morton is not "misusing instructional time by involving her students in her own political battle for gun control."

By this time, a state legislator who represents a nearby district has become aware of the children's efforts and visits their classroom to hear the whole story. He informs the students that he shares their concern and is willing to sponsor their bill in the upcoming legislative session. He makes several visits to the classroom to help the students draft the bill and prepare for their lobbying efforts. After some revisions, the bill becomes the first to pass through both houses in the legislative session, and the students are invited to the governor's signing.

Example #2
Performance Expectations: b, c, d, h, i

As a part of a unit on the powers and duties of the executive branch, Suzanne Kim gives her eighth-grade students a news article about President Clinton's process of appointing an Attorney General. Both of those whom he initially proposed found themselves in an awkward position because they had hired illegal immigrants (undocumented workers) to serve as babysitters for their children while they worked. Although most of the discussion in the articles is about the problems that women face in finding childcare, Kim wants her students to focus on the question "Who is a citizen and what does it take to become one?"

Kim passes out a list with the following on it:

Who is a citizen? How do you know?

1. A baby is born in Mexico while her parents, who are U.S. citizens, are on vacation. What is her citizenship?
2. A Jamaican woman has worked for many years in this country but has never applied for citizenship. This past year she married a U.S. citizen.
3. Refugees flee an oppressive, non-democratic government with which the United States has no diplomatic relations. The president tells the people of that nation that they can seek political asylum here. Are the refugees citizens? If not, are they eligible for citizenship?
4. Refugees flee an oppressive, non-democratic government with which the United States does have diplomatic relations. The president discourages these people from immigrating to the United States, saying that they are merely fleeing for economic purposes. Are these refugees citizens? If not, are they eligible to become citizens?

5. You emigrate to France. You have no intentions of returning to the United States. You no longer file U.S. income tax returns. Of which country are you a citizen?

6. A husband and wife have been undocumented workers in the United States for seven years. They have a baby. Is the baby a U.S. citizen?

Students work in small groups to discuss who is a citizen and what it takes to become a citizen. Kim arranges for a speaker from the Immigration and Naturalization Service to speak to her class the next day. Following this, the class analyzes current U.S. immigration policy in light of America's historical commitment to the ideals of justice and fairness.

Each student then writes an editorial appropriate for a specific newspaper of his or her choice, explaining the pros and cons of U.S. immigration policy and defending a position related to the policy. The editorials are evaluated on: accurate representation of contemporary immigration policy; the student's ability to analyze this policy in the light of the historical ideals and current practices discussed; development of a logical argument; and the student's success in choosing the appropriate tone for the selected newspaper.

Example #3
Performance Expectations: a, b, c, d, e, i, j

Students in Gary Huggett's eighth grade class become aware that the policies of Leading Edge, a national chain of stores that sells advanced electronic gadgets and sports equipment with great appeal to teenagers, discriminates against them because of their age. The students, led by Sara Berwick and Mike Holczer, decide that they are going to try to change the policy so that people under eighteen can go into a store without an adult chaperone.

Students research local, state, and national laws that relate to the situation and develop a plan to change the policy, which they then present to store officials. The students meet with the store manager, district manager, and finally the president of the company. The president writes a letter to each of the students announcing that she has changed the policy and teenagers will now be allowed to enter the store. Huggett asks each student to write an essay to answer the question: Has the student action accomplished its purpose? He asks students to defend the position they select with specific examples of action and legislation examined by the class during the study.

Six STANDARDS INTO PRACTICE: EXAMPLES FOR THE HIGH SCHOOL

① *Culture*

Social studies programs should include experiences that provide for the study of *culture and cultural diversity*, so that the learner can:

Performance Expectations   **Related Themes**

a. analyze and explain the ways groups, societies, and cultures address human needs and concerns;   **II III V**

b. predict how data and experiences may be interpreted by people from diverse cultural perspectives and frames of reference;   **II III IV V IX**

c. apply an understanding of culture as an integrated whole that explains the functions and interactions of language, literature, the arts, traditions, beliefs and values, and behavior patterns;   **II III V IX**

d. compare and analyze societal patterns for preserving and transmitting culture while adapting to environmental or social change;   **II III V**

e. demonstrate the value of cultural diversity, as well as cohesion, within and across groups;   **II III V IX**

f. interpret patterns of behavior reflecting values and attitudes that contribute or pose obstacles to cross-cultural understanding;   **II III IX**

g. construct reasoned judgments about specific cultural responses to persistent human issues;   **II III V IX**

h. explain and apply ideas, theories, and modes of inquiry drawn from anthropology and sociology in the examination of persistent issues and social problems.   **V**

FOCUS ON THE CLASSROOM: STANDARDS INTO PRACTICE

Example #1
Performance Expectations: b, c, e, f

"I don't see why we can't have prayer in school," says 17-year-old Marcus to his teacher, Bill Tate, and the rest of his U.S. Government class. "After all," continues Marcus, "every important document of this country makes reference to God. When a president or a judge is sworn in, they place their hands on the Bible. You place your hand on the Bible before you testify in court. What's the big deal?"

"What is the big deal?" Tate asks the class. "Marcus makes an interesting point."

"Well for me, the big deal is that I'm Buddhist," says Amy Wantanabe. "My concept of God and religion is probably different from what Marcus is talking about."

"Mine, too," said Saleem Hassan, "and Islam is the fastest growing religion in the world. What if Muslims become a religious majority in the U.S.? Which American principle would prevail, majority rule or freedom of religion?"

"I think 'freedom of religion' really means freedom from a state-imposed religion," said Marcia. "The big deal is that we live in a democracy not a theocracy, and even though God is mentioned in our documents and certain ceremonies, the public school shouldn't sanction any one form of religion."

Tate records the students' comments on the board in columns that represent positions that are either for or against religion in the schools. As he writes, more students chime in their opinions. Tate's primary role is keeping order to ensure that everyone is heard and no one's ideas are subjected to ridicule by other students. As the period draws to an end, Tate presents the students with a case study about a city's decision to have a nativity scene on public property. For homework, the students are to state which side of the argument they agree with and list all of the reasons with which they can support their opinions. In addition, they are to research analogous historical or contemporary situations.

In the next class session, students present their homework in small groups. Each group is given a recording sheet to list the points students make to support their opinions. The results are presented to the class and compared. Tate evaluates the individual assignments and group charts on the basis of the clarity of presentation and reasoning and the demonstrated understanding of the historical or contemporary comparisons used to support the argument.

Example #2

Performance Expectations: a, b, c, d

After reviewing basic patterns of economic activity and daily life in Mediterranean Europe at the time of Marco Polo, the students in June Smith's high school world history class prepare a general summary of the "world view" of that place and time. Smith then gives them an edited 20-page version of Marco Polo's account of his travels, with the assignment that they identify ways in which he reflects the world view of his time and information in his account that might challenge that world view.

The students are then asked to predict the impact of Marco Polo's story on the culture of his time. Next, Smith asks students to read the next section in their textbook to test their predictions. Following a class discussion of this reading, each student writes a paragraph summary of the impact of Marco Polo's story on the culture of his time and society and a second paragraph as it would have been written by people living in Mediterranean Europe from their own point of view.

⓫ *Time, Continuity, & Change*

Social studies programs should include experiences that provide for the study of *the ways human beings view themselves in and over time*, so that the learner can:

Performance Expectations	**Related Themes**
a. demonstrate that historical knowledge and the concept of time are socially influenced constructions that lead historians to be selective in the questions they seek to answer and the evidence they use;	Ⓘ ⒾⒾ Ⓥ
b. apply key concepts such as time, chronology, causality, change, conflict, and complexity to explain, analyze, and show connections among patterns of historical change and continuity;	ⒾⒾ Ⓥ ⓋⒾⒾ
c. identify and describe significant historical periods and patterns of change within and across cultures, such as the development of ancient cultures and civilizations, the rise of nation-states, and social, economic, and political revolutions;	Ⓘ Ⓥ ⓋⒾⒾ Ⓧ
d. systematically employ processes of critical historical inquiry to reconstruct and reinterpret the past, such as using a variety of sources and checking their credibility, validating and weighing evidence for claims, and searching for causality;	Ⓘ ⒾⒾ Ⓧ
e. investigate, interpret, and analyze multiple historical and contemporary viewpoints within and across cultures related to important events, recurring dilemmas, and persistent issues, while employing empathy, skepticism, and critical judgement;	Ⓘ ⒾⒾ Ⓥ ⓋⒾ ⓋⒾⒾ ⓋⒾⒾⒾ ⒾⓍ Ⓧ
f. apply ideas, theories, and modes of historical inquiry to analyze historical and contemporary developments, and to inform and evaluate actions concerning public policy issues.	Ⓥ ⓋⒾ ⓋⒾⒾ ⓋⒾⒾⒾ ⒾⓍ Ⓧ

FOCUS ON THE CLASSROOM: STANDARDS INTO PRACTICE

Example #1
Performance Expectations: a, b, c, d, e, f

Michael Roggart had been asked once too often "Why do we have to study this?" just as his twelfth grade Modern History class prepared to complete a study of the Bolshevik Revolution of 1917. The question caused him to think about how his students could gain a clearer understanding of what the Bolshevik Revolution meant in 1917 and what its significance is today for the peoples in the former Soviet Union and Eastern Europe. The student question was important, and Roggart's plan for a group assignment was designed to address it head on.

"Today," Roggart says, "I want you to prepare for group work we will be doing soon. Here are four accounts about causes of the Bolshevik Revolution of 1917 and whether or not it was justified. These include accounts written at the time of the Revolution from three different points of view—for, against, and undecided—and an account from a current textbook."

Roggart continues, "Analyze each document to determine the following:
a. what causes the writer emphasizes,
b. whether you can detect bias in the writer's presentation, and
c. the position the writer takes concerning revolution and the reasons for that position."

Roggert then tells the students, "After you have carefully analyzed the documents, *High School* assume the point of view of a person of that time period and develop your own position on the Bolshevik Revolution, providing reasons for your opinion. As you develop your position, keep this question in mind: When are people justified in revolting against an established government?"

The next day, Roggart asks students to divide into small groups to complete the following task:

a. Select a political event from recent history dealing with events in Russia, the Commonwealth of Independent States, or Eastern Europe, which appears to be a "revolution" by the criteria the class has previously established (using an accepted definition);

b. Determine how the event was viewed from two or more perspectives within the society affected by the revolution. Make certain the perspectives you choose have been written within five years of the revolution you are studying;

c. Determine how the event was viewed from two more perspectives outside of the target society;

d. Based upon your analysis of the sources in sections b and c, write an editorial taking a position on the event itself and whether this "revolution" is justified. Include reasons and evidence for your position, making comparisons and contrasts with the Bolshevik Revolution of 1917.

Roggart has asked the school's media center specialist to pull together several key resources for student use: news magazines related to the period in which the key events occurred; microfiches of newspapers; *Facts on File;* a CD-ROM disc of an encyclopedia; computer/laserdisc programs on the Cold War and beyond; and others. Some of these are made available in the classroom, others in the media center.

Some days after students have worked on the assignment, Roggart has the students sit in a circle and discuss their editorial positions. Prior to the beginning of class, the students have received photocopied packets of the editorials written by their peers for study and review. Roggart begins the discussion by restating the question: "Was your sample 'revolution' justified?" Students then present their views, critiquing one another as the discussion proceeds. Roggart has received the permission of the students to audiotape the discussion, and at its conclusion he makes a duplicate copy and forwards it to a history professor at a local college who has agreed to meet with the students after listening to the tape and reading copies of their editorials.

As a concluding activity, the professor visits the class and holds an extended discussion with students about their work. The professor critiques their positions, using the criteria applied by historians for making careful and valid judgments: credibility and reliability of sources, relevance of evidence employed, logical development of arguments, and impartiality of the analysis. The professor encourages the students to continue their investigations of these "revolutions" to determine if changes will be short-term or long-term.

High School

Example #2
Performance Expectations: a, d, e, f,

Within the scope of their study of World War II, John Ellis's tenth-grade students are examining the policies and actions employed by the German government to systematically destroy Jews and other groups of people in a campaign that has come to be known as the Holocaust. Many of Ellis's students are acquainted with the term "Holocaust" through exposure to popular culture, notably television and films. However, their understanding of the German government's policies from 1933 to 1945 is very limited, and Ellis decides to create an instructional unit focusing on the history of the Holocaust and its implications for contemporary society.

After providing the class with a chronology of events and trends during the period 1933–1945, Ellis asks students, "What questions do you want answered about the Holocaust, based upon the information you currently possess?" Students brainstorm their concerns and develop a list of questions for investigation. Ellis reviews the student questions and prepares instructional activities to address them and other topics that the students did not identify but which are crucial for establishing connections between the German government's policies for conducting war and those dedicated to systematic destruction of designated groups.

A number of the students' questions emphasize the human dimensions of the Holocaust. One student asks in class, "All I ever hear is how many people died, and I don't know what that really means. How did the people who were targeted deal with these policies?" Another student asks, "Did the victims resist, and if so how did they do it?" Questions such as these permit Ellis to develop strategies personalizing the study of the Holocaust. The next day he sets up a situation for student investigation. Posted on the chalkboard and on the classroom bulletin boards are nine artifact posters from the United States Holocaust Memorial Museum in Washington, D.C. Ellis has the students use a series of questions to analyze the posters, which depict artifacts in the museum's holdings. Among the artifacts pictured are photos of children killed in the Holocaust; shoes and suitcases confiscated by the German government and military during deportations and in concentration camps; stars, triangles, and other identification markings of targeted groups; and a range of other artifacts dealing with spiritual and physical resistance to the Holocaust, attempts to rescue targeted groups, and related topics.

Each student is assigned to a group to analyze three of the posters. As the students review the artifacts depicted, they analyze the artifacts for how they are related to the students' current state of knowledge about the Holocaust. They answer general questions such as "What do these artifacts tell you about the policies of the German government during the Holocaust?" and "What significance for personal action/behavior do these artifacts have?" as well as specific questions about the content of each poster. Once the students have completed their analyses, each group sends two representatives to other groups in the class to share their findings and gather information about the remaining six posters displayed in the room.

On the following day, the students report their findings to the class, using the artifact posters for reference. Other groups question and critique the findings of their peers, and Ellis facilitates the discussion by correcting inaccuracies and helping students construct careful, well-grounded generalizations. As the class period comes to a close, Ellis informs the students that their homework assignment is to read their textbook chapters on the history of the period 1933-45, keeping in mind the new information they have learned about the Holocaust from study of the artifact posters. They are then to revise the relevant sections of the textbook, rewriting them to reflect personal dimensions of the Holocaust that were not addressed by the textbook authors. Taking the position of experts, the students work in teams of two or three to complete this task, making sure that their revised text sections are historically accurate, clearly written, and comprehensive in their presentation of the difficulties encountered by targeted groups in this historical period. Once completed, the revised textbook sections are reviewed by a team of teachers and outside experts on the Holocaust, who provide feedback to the students in writing about their work.

Example #3

Performance Expectations: b, c, d, e, f

The annual celebration of Columbus Day is soon to occur in the school district and surrounding areas, and Anna Freire's ninth-grade world history class has been studying the period of European encounters with the Western Hemisphere. Beginning with the voyages of Norse peoples and continuing with study of the first European journeys to the Caribbean and North America, her students have been examining the reasons for these journeys of exploration and how the governments of Europe viewed the voyages as potential sources of revenue and wealth. During a class discussion about the planning for the voyages of Columbus, a student asks Freire, "What were the views of the peoples in the Americas about the Europeans? We don't ever hear their side of the story." Freire recognizes the need to pursue a balanced examination of this historical period. She responds, "That's an excellent question, one that is increasingly important to our understanding of this history. Here's how we will investigate your concern. As you know, Columbus Day has for some time been a holiday for the celebration of one view of this history, and often the voices of indigenous peoples have been minimized or silenced altogether. To provide an accurate and balanced perspective, we'll be investigating how all sides viewed this encounter."

To bring this topic to life, Freire brainstorms with the students a list of individuals and groups who would have a stake in the outcome of the encounters between Europeans and indigenous peoples in the Western Hemisphere. Among the individuals and groups they list are: European rulers, investors and traders from Europe, indigenous peoples and their rulers, indigenous religious leaders and officials, representatives of the Catholic church, military leaders of Europe, soldiers and sailors from Europe, and indigenous societies and European settlers. Freire divides the class into groups and assigns each group a person who represents a character for study. This character will be "brought to life" through individual research. The class will engage in

High School simulated discussions with the characters, discussing thematic questions about the encounters between Europeans and indigenous peoples. As an example, Freire tells the students, "Suppose I was Montezuma, leader of the Aztecs. In a discussion with the King of Spain and other representatives of European and indigenous societies, a core question might be: What are the key ideas that should form the basis of government in a society? This question is, on the surface, general, but everyone in the discussion group can respond to it based upon his or her world view and life history. Your research on your individual therefore needs to be thorough, accurate, and based upon substantial evidence of his or her actions or the actions of similar people in this time period."

After each student has been assigned a person for investigation, Freire places the students in discussion groups to make sure that diverse views are represented. Each group has a range of views, both European and indigenous, and with Freire's guidance, the groups develop a set of three core questions for discussion. Students prepare outlines of their positions for the discussions, and then present their discussions in character with the class and teacher as the audience. At the conclusion of each discussion, students from the audience ask questions of the historical characters to probe areas of their interest.

Freire evaluates the students' performance based upon their ability to develop an accurate, well-documented outline of their positions on the questions, their ability to remain within character during the discussion, and their effective use of discussion skills such as contributing, summarizing, questioning, and paraphrasing. After the group discussions have concluded, all students complete an essay on the question: "What have been the long-range historical implications of the European-indigenous peoples encounters?" Freire expects the papers to include examples of commentary provided during the group discussions and to fairly and accurately represent a range of viewpoints on the question.

Ⅲ *People, Places, & Environments*

Social studies programs should include experiences that provide for the study of *people, places, and environments*, so that the learner can:

Performance Expectations	Related Themes

a. refine mental maps of locales, regions, and the world that demonstrate understanding of relative location, direction, size, and shape; (IX)

b. create, interpret, use, and synthesize information from various representations of the earth, such as maps, globes, and photographs; (I) (II)

c. use appropriate resources, data sources, and geographic tools such as aerial photographs, satellite images, geographic information systems (GIS), map projections, and cartography to generate, manipulate, and interpret information such as atlases, data bases, grid systems, charts, graphs, and maps;

d. calculate distance, scale, area, and density, and distinguish spatial distribution patterns; (VIII) (IX)

e. describe, differentiate, and explain the relationships among various regional and global patterns of geographic phenomena such as landforms, soils, climate, vegetation, natural resources, and population; (VIII) (IX)

f. use knowledge of physical system changes such as seasons, climate and weather, and the water cycle to explain geographic phenomena; (VIII) (IX)

g. describe and compare how people create places that reflect culture, human needs, government policy, and current values and ideals as they design and build specialized buildings, neighborhoods, shopping centers, urban centers, industrial parks, and the like; (I) (II) (V) (VI) (VII)

h. examine, interpret, and analyze physical and cultural patterns and their interactions, such as land use, settlement patterns, cultural transmission of customs and ideas, and ecosystem changes; (I) (II) (VIII) (IX)

i. describe and assess ways that historical events have been influenced by, and have influenced, physical and human geographic factors in local, regional, national, and global settings; (I) (II) (VII) (IX)

j. analyze and evaluate social and economic effects of environmental changes and crises resulting from phenomena such as floods, storms, and drought; (V) (VII) (VIII)

k. propose, compare, and evaluate alternative policies for the use of land and other resources in communities, regions, nations, and the world. (V) (VII) (VIII) (IX) (X)

FOCUS ON THE CLASSROOM: STANDARDS INTO PRACTICE

Example #1
Performance Expectations: b, g, h, k

The problem presented to Nancy Gilligan's civics class is: Where will the new land-fill be located? The students have been studying how national issues and problems affect local communities. Now they have undertaken the task of finding solutions to a real community problem.

The students, working in small groups, are required to develop a set of criteria for examining potential landfill sites, determine the location of at least two available sites in their community, and assess those locations against their criteria. Each group presents arguments to support its decision to locate the landfill in a particular area. Such items as charts, videos, taped interviews with affected residents, and environmental impact projections are packaged into a multimedia production for class review and evaluation.

The group presentations are assessed on: strength of criteria used to make the decision; persuasiveness of presentation; accuracy and appropriateness of supporting data; and overall quality of the presentation.

Example #2
Performance Expectations: c, j

Vivian Lake is eager to see how well her senior contemporary world problems class will perform on the activity she has planned. She arranges the class into six groups of five students each. Each group member is assigned a number. Instead of a standard pencil and paper test of knowledge and recall, she asks the entire class to write position papers predicting the possible impact of an 8.0 earthquake on a rural Chinese village, the city of San Francisco, and Mexico City. The essays are to include a discussion of how the effects of this natural disaster will vary with population density, the built environment, and emergency response procedures. The students must predict possible death tolls and injuries, property damage, and approximate recovery time for the area. Each student is required to write an individual essay, but before doing a final draft the group members discuss each essay. The students then revise, edit, and rewrite their essays as a result of group discussion.

Lake plans to review the essays submitted by the students, and select one of the essays to represent each group. She has announced this process to the group so that they know that it is important for all of the essays submitted by the group members to be of high quality. She knows that this process encourages her students to think seriously about the quality of each of the other group members' essays as well as their own individual efforts.

Example #3
Performance Expectations: a, b, e, f, h, j

Marlon Gunter's world cultures class is studying Asia. Gunter uses a variety of maps to initiate the study of the region showing countries, physical features, climate regions, vegetation patterns, and population patterns. He typically highlights a phenomenon or characteristic for each major society that makes it distinctive in some way. For the study of India, he chooses the monsoon. He wants students to gain an understanding of the monsoon from an Indian perspective, so he searches for an Indian account of the monsoon experience. He finds just such an account in Raul Singh's *Kushwat Singh's India Without Humbug*. The account, which he reads to his students, defines monsoon as a season and describes the two monsoon seasons—winter and summer—and how Indians respond to them. The reading concludes:

> The monsoon is the most memorable experience in our lives. For others to know India and her people, they have to know the monsoon. It is not enough to read about it in books, or see it on the cinema screen,

or hear someone talk about it. It has to be a personal experience because nothing short of living through it can fully convey all it means to a people for whom it is not only the source of life, but also our most exciting impact with nature. What the four seasons of the year mean to the European, the one season of the monsoon means to the Indian. It is preceded by desolation; it brings with it the hopes of spring; it has the fullness of summer and the fulfillment of autumn all in one. . . .

Our attitude to clouds and rain remains fundamentally different from that of the Westerner. To the one, clouds are symbols of hope; to the other, of despair. The Indian scans the heavens and if nimbus clouds blot out the sun his heart fills with joy. The Westerner looks up and if there is no silver lining edging the clouds, his depression deepens. The Indian talks of someone he respects and looks up to as a great shadow, like the one cast by the clouds when they cover the sun. The Westerner, on the other hand, looks on a shadow as something evil and refers to people of a dubious character as shady types. For him, his beloved is like the sunshine and her smile a sunny smile. He escapes clouds and rain whenever he can seek summer climes. An Indian, when the rains come, runs out into the street shouting with joy and lets himself be soaked to the skin. (Singh, pp. 59–65)

An initial discussion follows in which students express a variety of personal views, such as: "I never thought about weather and climate as being that important"; "I don't think I could handle that way of life"; "We have droughts and floods in the U.S. too, but not in yearly patterns like that; it's one thing to get hit by an unexpected period of drought, or a tornado or something, but to know that every year you would go through the same extremes"; and "We have some of the same feelings when it is hot and dry or when it rains for long periods."

Gunter acknowledges their responses, sometimes probing for clarification or asking for evidence, but does not react either positively or negatively to students' positions. At the conclusion of the discussion, he writes the following statements on the board:

1.   To know India and its people, you have to know the monsoon through personal experience.
2.   Indians' attitudes about rain, clouds, and the weather are very different from those of Westerners.

He asks students to select one of the two statements and to write their reactions to it in a short essay of a page or so. He reads their essays, looking for a clear position statement, accurate description, and interpretation of the monsoon reading, use of other evidence, and sound reasoning.

Ⅳ *Individual Development & Identity*

Social studies programs should include experiences that provide for the study of *individual development and identity*, so that the learner can:

Performance Expectations	Related Themes

a. articulate personal connections to time, place, and social/cultural systems; ① ② ③ ⑨

b. identify, describe, and express appreciation for the influences of various historical and contemporary cultures on an individual's daily life; ① ② ③ ⑨

c. describe the ways family, religion, gender, ethnicity, nationality, socioeconomic status, and other group and cultural influences contribute to the development of a sense of self; ① ⑤

d. apply concepts, methods, and theories about the study of human growth and development, such as physical endowment, learning, motivation, behavior, perception, and personality;

e. examine the interactions of ethnic, national, or cultural influences in specific situations or events; ① ③ ⑨

f. analyze the role of perceptions, attitudes, values, and beliefs in the development of personal identity; ① ⑤

g. compare and evaluate the impact of stereotyping, conformity, acts of altruism, and other behaviors on individuals and groups; ① ⑤

h. work independently and cooperatively within groups and institutions to accomplish goals; ⑤ ⑩

i. examine factors that contribute to and damage one's mental health and analyze issues related to mental health and behavioral disorders in contemporary society. ⑤ ⑩

FOCUS ON THE CLASSROOM: STANDARDS INTO PRACTICE

Example #1
Performance Expectations: c, f

After a two-week unit on the influence of family and close friends on one's attitudes and beliefs and the means that social scientists use to gather information about such topics, Kendra Green provides her senior high school psychology students with an opportunity to demonstrate their understanding of how social scientists investigate such influences on people. Each student develops a series of interview questions with which to survey parents, siblings, grandparents, other family members, and close friends to identify their attitudes and values related to a current social issue; the student also develops a process for gathering survey data. Green works with students to avoid questions that might be offensive and to permit those interviewed to decline to answer if they so choose.

Following data collection, each student examines responses to determine the values and attitudes he or she shares with other family members and with close friends, and identifies possible ways in which family and friends have influenced the development of these values and attitudes. Each student writes a report comparing the attitudes and values of family and friends to his or her own and proposes hypotheses about the degree to which his or her attitudes and values have been learned from family and friends.

Green evaluates students' reports on the basis of their design of their interview questions, the process used in conducting the interviews, their data presentation and analysis, and appropriateness of their conclusions on the basis of data presented. She particularly looks for an examination of the relationship between the values of family and friends and the student's own positions on the selected social issues.

Example #2
Performance Expectations: c, f

The high school community service seminar meets twice a week to explore experiences participants are having in their two-hour-a-day community service placements. Each student has a placement that requires sustained interaction with the same person or group for the entire semester. Some class members serve in school-age daycare programs before and after the regular school day. Other placements are in a nursing home, where students work with the same residents for the semester. Still others assist in community education as long-term tutors of adult immigrants.

Students keep journals detailing their experiences. Seminar topics guide the content of the journal entries, and the entries are often the basis for group discussion.

During the second week of the course, Dr. James Lipide, a psychologist, presents a guest lecture on the topic of the lifelong development of positive self-identity. Over the next week, students observe and record in their journals incidents and practices that seem to enhance positive identity among the participants in the programs they are serving.

Students share their observations in a seminar discussion. Each student develops guidelines that he or she believes foster positive self-identity. These initial thoughts, a type of pre-test early in the service experience, are compared with a rewrite by each student as the course ends to determine whether the guidelines become more focused on positive personal identity and more closely linked to the group the student has assisted in his or her service project.

The group-developed guidelines are reviewed and reframed periodically during the course. They also serve as benchmarks in regularly structured self-assessments and in conference assessments with Edwina Cardinale, the instructor.

At the end of the course, each student is given the opportunity to rewrite the guidelines to reflect his or her individual experience and use his or her rewritten guidelines as the basis for an essay, "Building and Maintaining Positive Identity: A Lifelong Process." Cardinale reads each essay to determine: the application of student-developed guidelines (e.g., that there are many influences on the development of identity and that identity development is a lifelong process); and that the student's conclusion is drawn from the application of research to the volunteer experience.

High School

Example #3
Performance Expectations: a, b, c, d, f, g

Berry Richardson puts two statements on the chalkboard in his high school psychology class:

"The child is father to the man."

"As the twig is bent, so grows the tree."

He asks his students to form five small groups and discuss the meaning of the statements in terms of what they have learned in psychology class about the influence of family on the development of children. Each group is asked to create a story in which the attributes of the child are found in the adult. The stories are based upon historical figures. Richardson has available for the groups several biographical sketches that students can use in developing their stories.

After the stories are exchanged, students are asked to support or argue against the premise of the two statements on the chalkboard. The students develop several questions for discussion:

- Can people really change in later life?
- Are the first five years of life most important to a successful adult life?
- What influences a person's development?
- In what ways are children most likely to be like their parents?

To assess student learning, Richardson assigns each student to research the life of another historical or contemporary person and write a defense or rejection of the idea that the child gives an accurate picture of what the adult will be. The criteria for evaluation of the project include: stating a position clearly; defending the position with evidence from the lives of the historical parent and offspring; and relating examples to course content on the family's influence on developing children.

Ⓥ Individuals, Groups, & Institutions

Social studies programs should include experiences that provide for the study of *interactions among individuals, groups, and institutions,* so that the learner can:

Performance Expectations	Related Themes
a. apply concepts such as role, status, and social class in describing the connections and interactions of individuals, groups, and institutions in society;	Ⓘ Ⓘⓥ
b. analyze group and institutional influences on people, events, and elements of culture in both historical and contemporary settings;	Ⓘ Ⓘⓘ Ⓘⓥ Ⓥⓘ Ⓧ
c. describe the various forms institutions take, and explain how they develop and change over time;	Ⓘ Ⓘⓘ Ⓘⓥ Ⓥⓘ Ⓧ
d. identify and analyze examples of tensions between expressions of individuality and efforts used to promote social conformity by groups and institutions;	Ⓘ Ⓘⓘ Ⓘⓥ Ⓥⓘ Ⓧ
e. describe and examine belief systems basic to specific traditions and laws in contemporary and historical movements;	Ⓘ Ⓘⓘ Ⓥⓘ Ⓘⓧ
f. evaluate the role of institutions in furthering both continuity and change;	Ⓘ Ⓘⓘ Ⓥⓘ Ⓘⓧ Ⓧ
g. analyze the extent to which groups and institutions meet individual needs and promote the common good in contemporary and historical settings;	Ⓘ Ⓘⓘ Ⓥⓘ Ⓥⓘⓘ Ⓧ
h. explain and apply ideas and modes of inquiry drawn from behavioral science and social theory in the examination of persistent issues and social problems.	Ⓘ Ⓘⓘ Ⓥⓘ Ⓥⓘⓘ Ⓥⓘⓘⓘ Ⓘⓧ Ⓧ

FOCUS ON THE CLASSROOM: STANDARDS INTO PRACTICE

Example #1
Performance Expectations: a, b, c, d, e, f, g, h

Lori Pasqueriello's sociology students are tracing changes in social and family roles in the United States since the late nineteenth century. They examine the impact of political, economic, and cultural pressures that have influenced those changes. Students then select biographies of individuals who lived in different regions of the country during various time periods, and analyze the degree to which changes in social and political institutions (including the church, schools, political party, and organizations with which the individual was affiliated) appeared to both reflect and affect the individuals' career choices, values, and significant actions.

The students prepare oral presentations in which they describe the individual's various roles in his or her family, workplace, and other settings and how their roles were a reflection of both the times and personal choices of the individual. Students create graphics or collages that represent the individual and the institutions that influenced them. Effectiveness of research strategies and the quality of interpretation, analysis, and presentations serve as criteria for the teacher to evaluate evidence of understanding.

High School   **Example #2**
Performance Expectations: b, c, f, h

Students in Ardis Regan's U.S. history class have been examining how institutions change. As a culminating activity, she has the students brainstorm two lists: five major institutions and five major events of the twentieth century. This semester her class selects banks, schools, hospitals, the military, and their local government as the institutions for consideration. They choose the creation of the United Nations, the invention of the automobile, dropping the atomic bomb, the assassination of President Kennedy, and the breakdown of the Soviet Union as the five events. The students place the institutions and events on a grid.

	Banks	Schools	Hospitals	The Military	Local Government
Creation of the United Nations					
Invention of the automobile					
Dropping the atomic bomb					
Assassination of JFK					
Breakdown of the Soviet Union					

As students come into class the next day, they fill their names in one of the blocks and assume responsibility for researching the effects of the event on the institution and determining whether or not the institution had any influence on the event. After a week's research, the students share their findings. As a group, the class analyzes which institutions seemed to be more influenced by events, which seemed most resistant, and why this might be the case.

Regan has the students form groups by institution and prepare informational presentations that trace how their particular institution was affected by key events. The students discuss the form their presentations should take, choosing among a videotape, a "60 Minutes"-type television show, a feature article for their local paper, a cartoon pamphlet, and an informational pamphlet similar to those produced on a single issue by the League of Women Voters. Regan evaluates presentations on their accuracy, overall quality, and effectiveness in informing others.

Example #3

High School
Performance Expectations: a, b, d, e, f, g, h

Candidate Bill Clinton promised during the 1992 presidential campaign that if he became president, he would lift the ban on homosexuals in the military. If he did not, then the practice of asking recruits about their sexual preference before they enlisted and of expelling people if they were found to be homosexuals would continue.

During his first week in office, President Clinton announced he was issuing an executive order lifting the ban. Senator Nunn and Congressman Gingrich countered that they would introduce legislation that would continue the ban.

In George Willwerth's U.S. history class, students had just been discussing the life of Supreme Court Justice Thurgood Marshall and his contributions to civil rights in the United States. The discussion turns to civil rights and homosexuals.

One student comments, "What would happen if some soldier went to his or her commanding officer and said, 'I don't like working with a Hispanic soldier in my unit?' The commanding officer would tell the soldier to get a life."

Another adds, "And if someone went to the commanding officer and said, 'I don't like working with people who are Roman Catholic,' surely his commanding officer would have the same reaction."

A third student enters the conversation with, "Think what would happen if a man went in and complained that he didn't like being in a unit with women!"

"You people are nuts. You just don't think things through," shouts a female student. "We're talking about people sharing living quarters and taking showers in a common open space. You can't have gay people mixing with straight people like that."

Willwerth facilitates a student discussion about whether restrictions against homosexuals are the same as discrimination on the basis of gender, religion, ethnic background, and race. His role as facilitator involves maintaining order and courtesy, given the controversial nature of the subject. However, he recognizes the value of allowing students to share their thoughts and feelings in an academic setting where they also have the advantage of hearing a wide variety of viewpoints, thus strengthening an informed personal point of view.

To summarize the discussion, he asks students to consider their emerging viewpoints and be willing to stand by them for the time being, not letting peer pressures weaken their resolve, at least for the activity he is about to initiate. He then asks two students with clearly opposite points of view to represent the extremes of the argument and to form a human graph. Each states and briefly explains his or her position. Willwerth then asks the remaining students to take a position with or between the two "poles" at the place they feel best represents their point of view. He asks volunteers to articulate reasons for their position. Other students are allowed to change position if the newcomer has a good new point to add to the discussion.

Then, Willwerth asks each student to compose a letter, postcard, or telephone call to his or her member of Congress to clearly state his or her position on the matter and request the member's support for appropriate legislation if needed. Students are given the option of carrying through on the contact they initiated.

Ⅵ *Power, Authority, & Governance*

Social studies programs should include experiences that provide for the study of *how people create and change structures of power, authority, and governance,* so that the learner can:

Performance Expectations   **Related Themes**

a. examine persistent issues involving the rights, roles, and status of the individual in relation   (Ⅱ) (Ⅴ) (Ⅹ)
to the general welfare;

b. explain the purpose of government and analyze how its powers are acquired, used, and   (Ⅹ)
justified;

c. analyze and explain ideas and mechanisms to meet needs and wants of citizens, regulate   (Ⅴ) (Ⅶ) (Ⅸ) (Ⅹ)
territory, manage conflict, establish order and security, and balance competing conceptions
of a just society;

d. compare and analyze the ways nations and organizations respond to conflicts between   (Ⅰ) (Ⅱ) (Ⅴ)
forces of unity and forces of diversity;

e. compare different political systems (their ideologies, structure, institutions, processes, and   (Ⅱ) (Ⅲ) (Ⅴ) (Ⅸ)
political cultures) with that of the United States, and identify representative political leaders   (Ⅹ)
from selected historical and contemporary settings;

f. analyze and evaluate conditions, actions, and motivations that contribute to conflict and   (Ⅱ) (Ⅴ) (Ⅷ) (Ⅸ)
cooperation within and among nations;

g. evaluate the role of technology in communications, transportation, information-processing,   (Ⅶ) (Ⅷ) (Ⅸ)
weapons development, or other areas as it contributes to or helps resolve conflicts;

h. explain and apply ideas, theories, and modes of inquiry drawn from political science to   (Ⅰ) (Ⅱ) (Ⅴ) (Ⅷ)
the examination of persistent issues and social problems;   (Ⅸ) (Ⅹ)

i. evaluate the extent to which governments achieve their stated ideals and policies at home   (Ⅹ)
and abroad;

j. prepare a public policy paper and present and defend it before an appropriate forum in   (Ⅹ)
school or community.

FOCUS ON THE CLASSROOM: STANDARDS INTO PRACTICE

Example #1

Performance Expectations: a, h

Dan Kunitz begins class by having everyone stand up. Then he gives them directions: "Everyone who does not own property, sit down. Everyone who is not male, sit down. Everyone who is a part of a religion that is not Protestant or has no religion at all, sit down." When he has gone through a list that comprised the qualifications for voting in the 1788 election, no one is standing. He then divides the class into seven groups and sends them on a treasure hunt through the amendments to the U.S. Constitution to find all the amendments that have to do with voting and choosing a government. When they find Amendments 12, 15, 19, 22, 23, 24, and 26, Kunitz gives each group one amendment to analyze and to report their explanation to the whole class.

They then consider how various groups of people have gotten the right to vote. Finally, each group of students writes an amendment that will extend the right to vote to groups still not enfranchised, such as migrant workers and the homeless.

As a follow-up, the class selects the constitutions of six countries, and each group finds out how and when people secured the right to vote and how elections are held there.

In assessing the students' performance, Kunitz considers the completeness of the reports on the amendments, the accuracy of a timeline they prepare showing when various groups were enfranchised, the extent to which the key factors are explained in their amendment for the future inclusion of a group not yet enfranchised, and the accuracy of information on their chart comparing the U.S. Bill of Rights and rights statements from another country.

Example #2
Performance Expectations: a, b

The results of the 1990 election demanded redistricting within several states. John Hildebidle develops a lesson that goes beyond the traditional gerrymandering cartoon. He creates two interlocking activities. For the first activity, he arranges the student desks into eight groups of four each. As students enter the room, he asks them to line up in the back of the room. When they have done so, he asks: "Now, some of you are wearing striped shirts, and some of your T-shirts have colored sleeves, and one of you is wearing a plaid shirt. You each need to decide the predominant color you are wearing from the waist up and tell us." He continues, "Now we are going to make some important decisions today, and we are going to do that by table. You want your color to dominate as many tables as possible. You should sit down now with all of the others who are wearing your color." After much scrambling, the 32 ninth graders are distributed. Blue has twelve kids at three tables, white has nine at two with one student kneeling behind a desk, red has two tables of eight, and the rest have only one person per color.

When Yuk sees that each of the three students wearing odd colors is also wearing a white shirt under his or her sweater or sweatshirt, he urges, "Take off your sweater, and come on over here and join our group [white clothing] and we'll have as many people as the blues do." His logic prevails.

Two of the reds, sensing sure defeat and seeing no allies, and having blue shirts under their red sweaters, choose to take off their sweaters and quickly join the blues, giving them the majority again. Lucinda, one of the reds, notices that there are many people in the class wearing some sign of red and tries to start a red movement. She is shouted down by Ingrid, who tells her that she can't change the rules in midstream. Finally, Felix remembers that the rule is to predominate in a group and rearranges all the blues so that there are three of them at each table.

Hildebidle then tells the students that the group that has captured the most tables, now the blues, can decide which group goes to lunch first. Predictably they choose themselves.

The next day, Hildebidle hands out a pair of papers to each group. On the sheets are 100 letters, set up like a battleship. The letters are A, B, and C. The group's task

High School is to divide up the letters into districts. Each district has to have 10 letters in it, all letters have to be contiguous, and no letter can be isolated. The task is to make the As have the most districts, then the Bs, and then the Cs. The students draw their answers on transparencies so that they can share them with the class.

After all the groups have presented their maps, Hildebidle picks up on the questions he has heard students raising during their work, interspersing them with the main points of his lesson, making sure they talk about fairness, who makes the decision, and the effect of the decision upon the power of groups.

As a concluding evaluative activity, Hildebidle has his students write a plan that proposes a system for fair redistricting. Students must also evaluate the proposed system against criteria used in their state to establish voting districts. In assigning the task, Hildebidle asks students to reflect on the activities in the simulation and their subsequent decision. He plans to evaluate the essays on the basis of comprehensiveness and appropriateness of the plan to accomplish the goal, the use of relevant data, and application of external criteria (e.g., voting district requirements).

ⓋⅡ *Production, Distribution, & Consumption* *High School*

Social studies programs should include experiences that provide for the study of *how people organize for the production, distribution, and consumption of goods and services*, so that the learner can:

Performance Expectations **Related Themes**

a. explain how the scarcity of productive resources (human, capital, technological, and natural) requires the development of economic systems to make decisions about how goods and services are to be produced and distributed; (I) (III) (VI)

b. analyze the role that supply and demand, prices, incentives, and profits play in determining what is produced and distributed in a competitive market system; (V) (VI) (IX)

c. consider the costs and benefits to society of allocating goods and services through private and public sectors; (V) (VI)

d. describe relationships among the various economic institutions that comprise economic systems such as households, business firms, banks, government agencies, labor unions, and corporations; (V) (IX)

e. analyze the role of specialization and exchange in economic processes; (V) (VIII) (IX)

f. compare how values and beliefs influence economic decisions in different societies; (I) (IX)

g. compare basic economic systems according to how rules and procedures deal with demand, supply, prices, the role of government, banks, labor and labor unions, savings and investments, and capital; (I) (V) (VI) (IX)

h. apply economic concepts and reasoning when evaluating historical and contemporary social developments and issues; (I) (V) (VI)

i. distinguish between the domestic and global economic systems, and explain how the two interact; (IX)

j. apply knowledge of production, distribution, and consumption in the analysis of a public issue such as the allocation of health care or the consumption of energy, and devise an economic plan for accomplishing a socially desirable outcome related to that issue; (V) (VI) (VIII) (IX) (X)

k. distinguish between economics as a field of inquiry and the economy.

FOCUS ON THE CLASSROOM: STANDARDS INTO PRACTICE

Example #1
Performance Expectations: a, b, f, h, i, j

Clark Charkoudian's economics class is studying the relationship of price to supply and demand. He uses an informal lecture, rich with examples from daily experience and current world events, to illustrate the functions represented by standard supply, demand, and price curves to show how they are interrelated.

Students then apply this approach to the energy crisis of 1973. Students must deal with the results of the abrupt curtailment of supply and the sharp rise in prices. This exercise also provides an opportunity to review the concept of interdependence.

Students examine and relate numerous source materials, including: flow charts showing the source and end use of various kinds of energy used in the United States; a map showing the location of the world's proven oil reserves and its oil tanker routes; numerous charts showing petroleum supplies and gasoline and heating oil prices from 1972 to 1975; several newspaper stories about lines at service stations, gasoline rationing, the suspension of public events for lack of heat, etc. Students also consider policy proposals to deal with the crisis. Students make connections with individuals in the community who can describe this "crisis" in terms of their business and personal life experiences.

Students share the data they have collected in a variety of ways, and explore and take positions on alternative responses to the energy crisis. Each student adopts a policy position in response to the energy crisis and prepares a clearly written rationale for that position. Charkoudian examines and evaluates these position statements on the basis of the logic of the argument, the data used to support the position, and the impact the position is likely to have on the problem.

Example #2
Performance Expectations: b, h, j

Every election year Maria Santos begins the senior government class with an analysis of current political campaigns. Students explore and analyze candidate positions on the issues by organizing "truth squads," teams of four or five students who share their findings and conclusions with the rest of the class.

This year, most significant state and national campaign issues deal with economics: unemployment, taxes, trade, and incentives for resource development. These campaigns allow for the review and application of key concepts developed in previous units of study (e.g., regulation, incentives, resources, and taxes), as well as a focus on the role of values and beliefs in economic decision-making.

Santos reviews with the class key economic concepts in lively mini-lectures and brief readings. Students identify aspects of each of these concepts in the daily newspapers and weekly news magazines, prior to using them in the ongoing analysis of campaign issues.

A great deal of class time each week is devoted to research and analysis by the "truth squads." Santos meets with each group regularly. Each group periodically presents its findings and analyses to the class. Individuals maintain journals that record and explain group findings and analyses. Santos examines the journals to determine the campaign issues explored, the quality of the analyses in terms of the key economic concepts that relate to the issues, and the growing sophistication of the analyses over time.

Ⅷ *Science, Technology, & Society*

Social studies programs should include experiences that provide for the study of *relationships among science, technology, and society*, so that the learner can:

Performance Expectations	Related Themes
a. identify and describe both current and historical examples of the interaction and interdependence of science, technology, and society in a variety of cultural settings;	Ⅰ Ⅱ Ⅴ Ⅸ
b. make judgments about how science and technology have transformed the physical world and human society and our understanding of time, space, place, and human-environment interactions;	Ⅱ Ⅲ Ⅸ Ⅹ
c. analyze how science and technology influence the core values, beliefs, and attitudes of society, and how core values, beliefs, and attitudes of society shape scientific and technological change;	Ⅰ Ⅱ Ⅲ Ⅴ Ⅵ Ⅶ Ⅸ Ⅹ
d. evaluate various policies that have been proposed as ways of dealing with social changes resulting from new technologies, such as genetically engineered plants and animals;	Ⅱ Ⅵ Ⅸ Ⅹ
e. recognize and interpret varied perspectives about human societies and the physical world using scientific knowledge, ethical standards, and technologies from diverse world cultures;	Ⅰ Ⅱ Ⅲ Ⅴ Ⅸ Ⅹ
f. formulate strategies and develop policies for influencing public discussions associated with technology-society issues, such as the greenhouse effect.	Ⅴ Ⅵ Ⅹ

FOCUS ON THE CLASSROOM: STANDARDS INTO PRACTICE

Example #1

Performance Expectations: a, c, d, e, f

Don Crowley's law in society class begins a new mock trial. In this case, the captain of the high school swim team has been accused of date rape. The alleged victim is the captain of the girl's swim team. The two have been friends since childhood, dated briefly, and broke up, although they had agreed to remain friends. Since both were dateless for the prom, they decided to go together. At an after-prom party at a friend's house, both had too much to drink. Lisa went upstairs, intending to go to the bathroom, and John misdirected her into the bedroom of the absent parents, where the rape allegedly took place. At the hospital, Lisa is examined, and a semen sample collected.

The crucial evidence in this case revolves around DNA testing. Charlotte Thompson, the science teacher teaming with Crowley on this project, arranges for a scientist to visit the class to explain and lead a discussion about DNA "fingerprinting." Students are amazed to learn that, like fingerprints, no two people have the same DNA and that each DNA molecule can be stretched out to three feet for analysis.

Students research the law in the matter. They find out which states allow DNA "fingerprinting" results in court and which do not. They find that there is no Supreme Court ruling yet, and that their state has a spotty record for allowing DNA evidence in rape cases. After studying the situation, the class decides that there is good scientific evidence of reliability and that the test results should be admitted. Not only does this affect the outcome of the mock trial; it sparks student interest in supporting the use of DNA results in their state's court system. They meet with their state representative, draft legislation, develop a plan to lobby for their cause, and testify on its behalf at a legislative hearing. Throughout this unit, students keep journals.

As a culminating activity, each student prepares an essay evaluating the process he or she employed and its relationship to policymaking. Crowley and Thompson evaluate each essay for credit in both of their classes on these factors: clarity of representation of strategies taken; ability to critique strategies for their effectiveness, including self-criticism concerning strategies each had advocated; and an understanding of scientific principles involved.

In addition, Crowley and Thompson evaluate each student's draft of legislation and each student's lobbying plan for form and clarity. They also read each student's journal, making comments and raising questions, giving credit for completion but not grading it for quality. In their subsequent reflection on their joint-teaching effort, both teachers are pleased that students gained a better understanding of the relationship among science, technology, and society, while also having the experience of participating in the political process to help bring about social change.

Example #2

Performance Expectations: a, c, e, f

Rebecca Moore's ninth grade social studies class has been looking at questions about how technology affects society and how to make reasoned decisions about questions dealing with scarcity and the common good.

She has divided the class into groups and given each a set of character cards presenting four different people awaiting a liver transplant. Each of the people in the dilemma is a good match for the available liver. The students realize that the people they do not choose may die before other suitable donors can be found. The candidates for the transplant are:

1. An 18-year-old female accident victim who is a smoker and recent recipient of a full scholarship to Northwestern University.
2. A 36-year-old mother of two, currently serving time in prison for refusing to reveal the whereabouts of her children, contending that her ex-husband has abused them.
3. The popular 61-year-old male mayor of a large southwestern city who also needs a heart transplant.
4. A 47-year-old doctor who practices in a walk-in clinic in a low socio-economic urban area serving a multicultural population.

Each group has two major tasks. First, its members must decide how to decide. The person sitting closest to the clock writes down the factors the group considers in making the decision. Then the group chooses the recipient of the liver and develops an explanation of how they reached that decision. The group has to pick the three top factors, by consensus or by vote. The person sitting closest to the pencil sharpener reports the group's process and decision to the class. As they report, the teacher notes their reasons on the overhead projector.

To assess students' comprehension of the dilemma and the task process and outcomes, Moore has the students categorize the factors the entire class has considered in reaching a decision. Additionally, she has them write about how they reached their decision and how other people's ideas influenced that decision. As she reads the papers, she looks for logical clarity and consistency in the way the students construct the explanation of their decision.

Example #3
Performance Expectations: a, c, e, f

Nancy Makepeace's high school law and justice class has been looking in depth at the Bill of Rights. They are currently examining freedom of the press and how changes in policies and practices related to electronic media technology could have implications for the future of this freedom. Makepeace decides to use the media treatment of a current criminal case that has yet to go to trial to illustrate how television can pit this freedom of the press against another constitutional right—that of a fair and speedy trial.

Makepeace assigns the students to cooperative learning groups and gives them a week to build a case, complete with documentation, either for or against this statement: "Advances in mass media technology will eventually force us to limit freedom of the press." Meanwhile, Makepeace strategically places around the classroom a number of newspapers and news magazines that feature stories about the case. Students often borrow and use such material to write current events reports for extra credit. Makepeace also videotapes news reports related to the case and plays these as background as the students work. Several students pick up on the barrage of information they are being subjected to about the case and make comments or raise questions, but Makepeace deflects their comments and queries, saying she is providing this information to help students with their task.

In fact, Makepeace has set the stage for the following Monday, at which time she announces that every member of the class has been called for jury duty and is thus a member of the pool of potential jurors for the trial related to the criminal case they have been possibly inadvertently following. After a discussion of what this means, there is much chatter about the details of the case. Many students quickly realize that there is much variation in the amount of information students have absorbed—and much discrepancy about the "facts" of the case. Makepeace has contacted two local attorneys who appear and take students through voir dire proceedings for jury selection. A lively discussion follows in which students, teacher, and attorneys deliberate current policies and practices of mass media, the power of it to influence public thinking, and the effects of this on individual rights.

Two questions dominate and form the basis for the assessment Makepeace develops to follow-up this week-long activity: Is a fair trial possible when a case has received national attention? How has media technology changed the issues surrounding freedom of the press, and what direction is needed? The students, working in pairs, develop pro/con editorials on the first topic. To assess achievement, Makepeace evaluates the completeness of each student's prewriting assignment and a required pro/con chart,

High School   checking for information provided by the attorneys. She also assesses the quality of their editorials, looking for a clearly stated position supported by evidence and logic.

As a follow-up application, she sets up a point/counterpoint discussion which the students tape. In each group of three students, one presents an introductory piece explaining the issue of freedom of the press and complications resulting from technology, including a timeline of media developments over the last fifty years that have an impact on freedom of the press. The other two students present a point/counterpoint discussion about the direction which the United States needs to take. Makepeace evaluates the performance of each student through his or her taped presentation or script.

IX Global Connections

Social studies programs should include experiences that provide for the study of *global connections and interdependence*, so that the learner can:

Performance Expectations	Related Themes
a. explain how language, art, music, belief systems, and other cultural elements can facilitate global understanding or cause misunderstanding;	I II III
b. explain conditions and motivations that contribute to conflict, cooperation, and interdependence among groups, societies, and nations;	V VI
c. analyze and evaluate the effects of changing technologies on the global community;	VIII
d. analyze the causes, consequences, and possible solutions to persistent, contemporary, and emerging global issues, such as health, security, resource allocation, economic development, and environmental quality;	V VI VIII
e. analyze the relationships and tensions between national sovereignty and global interests, in matters such as territory, economic development, nuclear and other weapons, use of natural resources, and human rights concerns;	VI VII VIII
f. analyze or formulate policy statements demonstrating an understanding of concerns, standards, issues, and conflicts related to universal human rights;	X
g. describe and evaluate the role of international and multinational organizations in the global arena;	V VII
h. illustrate how individual behaviors and decisions connect with global systems.	IV V

FOCUS ON THE CLASSROOM: STANDARDS INTO PRACTICE

Example #1
Performance Expectations: d, f, g, h

Tip Jimenez, as leader of the economics section of his ninth grade civics course, wants students to recognize the United States' economic interdependence with other nations, but also wants them to consider the larger question of whether this interdependence ever leads to worker exploitation, how exploitation might be defined, and what the relationship is between exploitation and human rights. To set the stage, he shares the lyrics of a song by the social and political activist group Sweet Honey in the Rock. This song is the story of a woman who purchases a blouse from a U.S. department store, then traces its origins to workers, crops, and resources throughout the world. The song attempts to have listeners raise questions regarding their own complicity as consumers in the exploitation of workers and resources. Ending with the question "Are my hands clean?" the song addresses how our wants and needs are often met at the expense of others.

Jimenez has students check their outer garments and shoes to determine countries of origin. Marking the wall map to illustrate data gathered provides students a visual display on which to analyze leading trading partners in the garment industry. The more difficult challenge is for students to research and create a database of wage information for the various countries identified as sources, including the United States. The database is used to compare wages and costs of living in various parts of the world, in order to address the question raised in the song. Jimenez assesses the students' work for accuracy, relevance, currency of data, and ability to generate inquiry questions using the data.

Example #2
Performance Expectations: b, d, e, f

In his tenth grade world civilizations class, Anthony Owens's students are examining post-World War II Europe. The concepts of nationalism and collective security are emphasized as a perennial point of tension among neighboring nations, a point well illustrated in the region under study. Owens poses this problem to the class: How can peace and security best be maintained in Europe during the last decade of the twentieth century?

Students discuss related concepts and questions before embarking on problem-solving, including: What tensions currently threaten efforts at European unity? What national interests should be preserved in an integrated Europe? How can European states respond to issues such as nuclear proliferation, international terrorism, and population migration, including refugees? From these questions, Owens has students select one they feel is critical to the larger question and on which they wish to focus their problem-solving efforts.

Owens presents a variety of options to the students, so they can demonstrate understanding of the relevant concepts, issues, and appropriate problem-solving strategies. Then, either individually or in groups, students write essays, present panel discussions or debates, develop poster exhibits, or create multimedia programs to share the solutions they have developed. Owens assesses the students' work based upon the thoroughness of their research, their analysis of the key issues involved, and the quality of their presentations.

Example #3
Performance Expectations: a, f

In a number of units in her world history course, Glory Ann Fitzpatrick has found that her students become quite agitated by incidents in which rights have been violated. Thus, for a week, Fitzpatrick focuses on the topic of universal human rights by having students reflect on the incidents they have noted and then, in small groups, develop a list of rights they believe all human beings should have, regardless of where they live or their ethnicity, gender, or religion. They bring these back to the larger group and, by consensus, compile a single list from each group's contributions. They then attempt to prioritize these, defining which are essential and non-essential to survival. Students develop written rationales for each right, justifying its inclusion on the list. As a final check, Fitzpatrick asks students to re-evaluate each right in terms of whether it is appropriate across all cultures and time periods they have studied in the course. Where irreconcilable differences among students occur with regard to the universality of the right, students are given the option to present a minority report. She then distributes the Universal Declaration of Human Rights, and has them, working in small groups, compare their work with that of the United Nations. Students find differences, but note that many have to do with current conditions that seem to have changed since the earlier document was written.

As a follow-up activity, Fitzpatrick has students hypothesize about which human rights would be the easiest and most difficult to guarantee in the United States for all residents. This exercise serves as a prelude to library and community research about the relationship between human rights "guaranteed" in various treaties and actual practices of governments.

Using excerpts from a variety of media about selected world societies, Fitzpatrick's students conduct research independently and create and mount a public display regarding the protection and violation of human rights. This display evaluates the record of various governments against recognized international standards, e.g., the Universal Declaration of Human Rights, the International Covenants of Civil and Political Rights, the Convention on the Prevention of Genocide, and the United Nations Convention on the Rights of the Child.

Fitzpatrick assesses individual and collaborative student work according to its completeness, evidence of understanding the concept of universal human rights, and skill in evaluating government policies related to the international standards.

Example #4
Performance Expectations: b, d, f

Kevin Pobst teaches the senior capstone social studies course in his high school called "Worldwise." In this course, he uses a variety of primary and secondary sources to address current issues and examine current events as they unfold. One facet of his course syllabus calls for students to research current issues in the *Congressional Record* to identify an international issue in which factions within the United States and factions within another country take different positions, e.g., using the United States military to take food and supplies to groups within nations against the will of those in power.

Pobst divides the students into teams representing the conflicting points of view within each country. Each team prepares a list of critical concerns from their particular vantage point regarding the issue. After completing their research, each group determines the best possible solution for all concerned and then predicts the actual outcome, providing a rationale for their own solution and reasons why they predicted the outcome they did. As a follow-up, students follow events that determine the actual outcome and compare their prediction to reality.

The criteria for evaluation include the degree to which suggested and predicted solutions and rationale are reasoned, thoroughly researched or treated, pertinent, and effectively argued; these will give Pobst evidence that students understand the roots and issues of, and possible solutions to, international conflict.

 **X** *Civic Ideals and Practices*

Social studies programs should include experiences that provide for the study of *the ideals, principles, and practices of citizenship in a democratic republic*, so that the learner can:

Performance Expectations	**Related Themes**

a. explain the origins and continuing influence of key ideals of the democratic republican form of government, such as individual human dignity, liberty, justice, equality, and the rule of law;   **Ⅱ Ⅴ Ⅵ**

b. identify, analyze, interpret, and evaluate sources and examples of citizens' rights and responsibilities;   **Ⅱ**

c. locate, access, analyze, organize, synthesize, evaluate, and apply information about selected public issues—identifying, describing, and evaluating multiple points of view;   **Ⅰ Ⅱ Ⅴ Ⅸ**

d. practice forms of civic discussion and participation consistent with the ideals of citizens in a democratic republic;   **Ⅱ Ⅴ Ⅵ**

e. analyze and evaluate the influence of various forms of citizen action on public policy;   **Ⅰ Ⅴ Ⅵ**

f. analyze a variety of public policies and issues from the perspective of formal and informal political actors;   **Ⅴ Ⅵ**

g. evaluate the effectiveness of public opinion in influencing and shaping public policy development and decision-making;   **Ⅱ Ⅴ Ⅵ Ⅸ**

h. evaluate the degree to which public policies and citizen behaviors reflect or foster the stated ideals of a democratic republican form of government;   **Ⅳ Ⅴ Ⅵ**

i. construct a policy statement and an action plan to achieve one or more goals related to an issue of public concern;   **Ⅴ Ⅵ**

j. participate in activities to strengthen the "common good," based upon careful evaluation of possible options for citizen action.   **Ⅴ Ⅵ**

FOCUS ON THE CLASSROOM: STANDARDS INTO PRACTICE

Example #1
Performance Expectations: c, e, h

The city of Wexford was reeling from a riot that had taken place after an unpopular verdict regarding charges of a police beating of a Latino motorist. Several witnesses had testified that the police used unnecessary force in taking the man into custody. He had suffered numerous broken bones and severe head injuries and was in critical condition on a respirator in the county hospital. The jury in this case found the evidence lacking and acquitted the police officer. The city erupted in violence. Homes, stores, and shops were looted and burned. Several people were killed, and hundreds more were injured. The police and later the National Guard were called in to restore order. Wexford was changed in ways never imagined.

At Wexford High School, the riot is the only thing on people's minds. Everyone knows at least one person who was directly affected by what happened. Most teachers spend some time talking about it. They encourage students to express their thoughts and feelings. As soon as possible, many teachers return students to the work they were doing before the riot.

Larry Hudson has a different idea. He doesn't want the students to think of the riot as an isolated incident. He wants to place it in the broader context of power, authority, and governance and civic ideals and practice. On the chalkboard he lists the following: Shays' rebellion, Nat Turner's slave rebellion, the Red Summer, the Homestead strike, Ole Miss, and the Watts riot.

As the students enter Hudson's public issues class, they look at the board with puzzlement. "What's this about, Mr. Hudson?" Juan Rivera asks.

"Well," Hudson answers, "we're going to try to see how people have resorted to riot and rebellion at various points in our nation's history as a form of redress of grievances. Also, we're going to ask ourselves whether or not riot or rebellion is ever justified and whether or not the costs outweigh the benefits. We will need to draw on what you learned about what happened in Wexford last week and what you can learn from history to try to answer these questions. As an assignment, you need to collect newspaper, television, news magazine, and personal accounts of what happened here to compare it with research you do on one of the riots or rebellions I have listed on the board. We want to know the background of the historical event, key people, multiple points of view about it, catalyst or starting event or incident, consequences, and resolution."

Each student selects one of the historical events and prepares a data retrieval chart to address the questions in the assignment. As an in-class assessment, Hudson asks each student to use the data from the chart to write an editorial comparing the historical event with the incident in Wexford. Hudson plans to assess the accuracy of the descriptions of the events and the logical support students offer for similarities and differences between the events.

Example #2
Performance Expectations: a, b, c, d, f

Nico Bellini's eleventh grade contemporary American issues class is concluding a unit on the Bill of Rights. Nancy enters class complaining about the musical lyrics and language she hears regularly on the radio; she deems some of it offensive to females and thinks a law should be passed to stop it. Her friend Maria disagrees with Nancy, noting that it is difficult to legislate restrictions on some area of expression without endangering the freedom of expression for all. Their classmate Joe responds by saying, "This isn't about freedom of expression; it's about maintaining standards of morality in our society which are slipping fast."

Overhearing this discussion, Bellini comments, "It's interesting that all of you are discussing this issue today, because that's one of the most contentious dilemmas related to the First Amendment in our society." A number of students in the class suggest that for their concluding unit project, they investigate the viewpoints of experts and community residents and conduct a public community forum on this issue.

High School   Bellini listens carefully to the views of the students, and after a lengthy discussion, poses this problem for student investigation: Are limits on freedom of expression appropriate in our democratic society?

Students have previously studied the relationship of state authority to individual rights in the United States, notably in Supreme Court decisions. Based upon their prior work, the students select a variety of judicial case studies for exploration that illustrate different responses to the problem. They also review historical Supreme Court decisions containing precedents (i.e., "clear and present danger" and others), which have influenced subsequent judicial rulings in First Amendment cases.

Students work in small groups to develop their presentations, and with Bellini's guidance refine their positions to highlight possible solutions to the problem and implications for behavior arising from these proposed solutions. They hold a forum in their class to identify three clearly different positions, to examine the pros and cons of each, and to discuss the consequences of implementing each of the positions. Excited about their own classroom forum, the students agree to organize and publicize to the community a public forum, keeping in mind that while no consensus may be reached at the public forum, a more informed public discussion of the problem and proposed solutions is clearly possible.   Students also prepare audiovisual materials illustrating the key points of their perspectives, supporting their key points with research findings.

As a follow-up assessment, Bellini asks each student to create a political cartoon illustrating the pros, cons, and consequences of their own preferred position on limiting freedom of expression.

REFERENCES

References

Buscaglia, Leo. *The Fall of Freddy the Leaf: A Story of Life for All Ages.* New York: Holt, Reinhart & Winston, 1982.

Coerr, E. *Sadako and the Thousand Paper Cranes.* New York: Bantam Doubleday Dell Publishing Group, 1977.

Collier, J. L. *My Brother Sam Is Dead.* New York: Four Winds Press, 1974.

De Angeli, M. *Door in the Wall.* New York: Doubleday, 1989.

Di Salvo-Ryan, D. *Uncle Willie and the Soup Kitchen.* New York: Morrow Jr. Books, 1991.

Forbes, Esther. *Johnny Tremain.* New York: F. Watts, 1943.

Greer, G., and Ruddick, B. *Max and Me and the Time Machine.* San Diego: Harcourt Brace, Jovanovich, 1988.

Jefferson, Thomas. *Notes on the State of Virginia.* New York: Harper & Row, 1964; reprint of 1861 edition.

Lowry, L. *Number the Stars.* New York: Bantam Doubleday Dell Publishing Group, 1989.

Mata, C. *Daniel's Story.* New York: Scholastic, 1993.

McGuffy, W. H. *McGuffy Reader.* Washougal, Wash.: Moore Learning Systems, 1983.

McKissack, P. C., and J. Pinkney. *Mirandy and Brother Wind.* New York: Knopf, 1988.

McSwigan, Marie. *Snow Treasure.* New York: E. P. Dutton & Co., 1942.

Roop, P., and C. Roop. *Ahyoka and the Talking Leaves.* New York: Lathrop, Lee & Shepard, 1992.

Singh, R., ed. *Kushwat Singh's India without Humbug.* Bombay: India Book House, 1977.

Stowe, Harriet Beecher. *Uncle Tom's Cabin.* New York: Coward, McCann & Geoghegan, 1929.

United States Holocaust Memorial Council. *Artifact Poster Set.* Washington, D.C.: United States Holocaust Memorial Council, 1993.

Appendix A **ESSENTIAL SKILLS FOR SOCIAL STUDIES**

Essential Skills for Social Studies: Acquiring Information

Suggested strength of instructional effort ◖ Minimum ◗ Some ◕ Major ● Intense

Appendix A

Grade-level columns for all skill ratings: **K-3, 4-6, 7-9, 10-12**

A. Reading Skills

1. Comprehension
- Read to get literal meaning
- Use chapter and section headings, topic sentences, and summary sentences to select main ideas
- Differentiate main and subordinate ideas
- Select passages that are pertinent to the topic studied
- Interpret what is read by drawing inferences
- Detect cause and effect relationships
- Distinguish between the fact and opinion; recognize propaganda
- Recognize author bias
- Use picture clues and picture captions to aid comprehension
- Use literature to enrich meaning
- Read for a variety of purposes: critically, analytically, to predict outcomes, to answer a question, to form an opinion, to skim for facts
- Read various forms of printed material: books, magazines, newspapers, directories, schedules, journals

2. Vocabulary
- Use usual word attack skills: sight recognition, phonetic analysis, structural analysis
- Use context clues to gain meaning
- Use appropriate sources to gain meaning of essential terms and vocabulary: glossary, dictionary, text, word lists
- Recognize and understand an increasing number of social studies terms

3. Rate of Reading
- Adjust speed of reading to suit purpose
- Adjust rate of reading to difficulty of the material

B. Study Skills

1. Find Information
- Use various parts of a book (index, table of contents, etc.)
- Use key words, letters on volumes, index, and cross references to find information
- Evaluate sources of information—print, visual, electronic
- Use appropriate source of information
- Use the community as a resource

2. Arrange Information in Usable Forms
- Make outline of topic
- Prepare summaries
- Make timelines
- Take notes
- Keep records
- Use italics, marginal notes, and footnotes
- Listen for information
- Follow directions
- Write reports and research papers
- Prepare a bibliography

C. Reference & Information-Search Skills

1. The Library
- Use card catalog to locate books
- Use *Reader's Guide to Periodical Literature* and other indexes
- Use COMCATS (Computer Catalog Service)
- Use public library telephone information service

2. Special References
- Almanacs
- Encyclopedias
- Dictionary
- Indexes
- Government publications
- Microfiche
- Periodicals
- News sources: newspapers, news magazines, TV, radio, videotapes, artifacts

3. Maps, Globes, Graphics
Use map- and globe-reading skills
- Orient a map and note directions
- Locate places on map and globe
- Use scale and compute distances
- Interpret map symbols and visualize what they mean
- Compare maps and make inferences
- Express relative location
- Interpret graphs
- Detect bias in visual material
- Interpret social and political messages of cartoons
- Interpret history through artifacts

4. Community Resources
- Use sources of information in the community
- Conduct interviews of individuals in the community
- Use community newspapers

D. Technical Skills Unique to Electronic Devices

1. Computer
- Operate a computer using prepared instructional or reference programs
- Operate a computer to enter and retrieve information gathered from a variety of sources

2. Telephone and Television Information Networks
- Ability to access information through networks

From "In Search of a Scope and Sequence for Social Studies." *Social Education*, 53(6), October 1989, 376-385. This is part of a report of the NCSS Task Force on Scope and Sequence.

Essential Skills for Social Studies: Organizing & Using Information

Suggested strength of instructional effort ◓ Minimum ◑ Some ◕ Major ● Intense

Appendix A

K-3 4-6 7-9 10-12

A. Thinking Skills

1. Classify Information
....Identify relevant factual material
....Sense relationship between items of factual information
....Group data in categories according to appropriate criteria
....Place in proper sequence:
(1) order of occurrence
(2) order of importance
....Place data in tabular form: charts, graphs, illustrations

2. Interpret Information
....State relationships between categories of information
....Note cause and effect relationships
....Draw inferences from factual material
....Predict likely outcomes based on factual information
....Recognize the value dimension of interpreting factual material
....Recognize instances in which more than one interpretation of factual material is valid

3. Analyze Information
....Form a simple organization of key ideas related to a topic
....Separate a topic into major components according to appropriate criteria
....Examine critically relationships between and among elements of a topic
....Detect bias in data presented in various forms: graphics, tabular, visual, print
....Compare and contrast credibility of differing accounts of the same event

4. Summarize Information
....Extract significant ideas from supporting illustrative details
....Combine critical concepts into a statement of conclusions based on information
....Restate major ideas of a complex topic in concise form

K-3 4-6 7-9 10-12

....Form opinion based on critical examination of relevant information
....State hypotheses for further study

5. Synthesize Information
....Propose a new plan of operation, create a new system, or devise a futuristic scheme based on available information
....Reinterpret events in terms of what *might* have happened, and show the likely effects on subsequent events
....Present visually (chart, graph, diagram, model, etc.) information extracted from print
....Prepare a research paper that requires a creative solution to a problem
....Communicate orally and in writing

6. Evaluate Information
....Determine whether or not the information is pertinent to the topic
....Estimate the adequacy of the information
....Test the validity of the information, using such criteria as source, objectivity, technical correctness, currency

B. Decision-Making Skills
....Identify a situation in which a decision is required
....Secure needed factual information relevant to making the decision
....Recognize the values implicit in the situation and the issues that flow from them
....Identify alternative courses of action and predict likely consequences of each
....Make decision based on the data obtained
....Take action to implement the decision

C. Metacognitive Skills
....Select an appropriate strategy to solve a problem
....Self-monitor one's thinking process

Essential Skills: Interpersonal Relationships & Social Participation

K-3 4-6 7-9 10-12

A. Personal Skills
....Express personal convictions
....Communicate own beliefs, feelings, and convictions
....Adjust own behavior to fit the dynamics of various groups and situations
....Recognize the mutual relationship between human beings in satisfying one another's needs

B. Group Interaction Skills
....Contribute to the development of a supportive climate in groups
....Participate in making rules and guidelines for group life
....Serve as a leader or follower
....Assist in setting goals for the group

K-3 4-6 7-9 10-12

....Participate in delegating duties, organizing, planning, making decisions, and taking action in group setting
....Participate in persuading, compromising, debating, and negotiating in the resolution of conflicts and differences

C. Social and Political Participation Skills
....Keep informed on issues that affect society
....Identify situations in which social action is required
....Work individually or with others to decide on an appropriate course of action
....Work to influence those in positions of social power to strive for extensions of freedom, social justice, and human rights
....Accept and fulfill social responsibilities associated with citizenship in a free society

From "In Search of a Scope and Sequence for Social Studies." *Social Education,* 53(6), October 1989, 376-385. This is part of a report of the NCSS Task Force on Scope and Sequence.

Appendix B **DEMOCRATIC BELIEFS AND VALUES**

Democratic Beliefs and Values

A. *Rights of the Individual*
Right to life
Right to liberty
Right to dignity
Right to security
Right to equality of opportunity
Right to justice
Right to privacy
Right to private ownership of property

B. *Freedoms of the Individual*
Freedom to participate in the political process
Freedom of worship
Freedom of thought
Freedom of conscience
Freedom of assembly
Freedom of inquiry
Freedom of expression

C. *Responsibilities of the Individual*
To respect human life
To respect the rights of others
To be tolerant
To be honest
To be compassionate
To demonstrate self-control
To participate in the democratic process
To work for the common good
To respect the property of others

D. *Beliefs Concerning Societal Conditions and Governmental Responsibilities*
Societies need laws that are accepted by the majority of the people.
Dissenting minorities are protected.
Government is elected by the people.
Government respects and protects individual rights.
Government respects and protects individual freedoms.
Government guarantees civil liberties.
Government works for the common good.

Source: John Jarolimek, Chair, NCSS Task Force on Scope and Sequence. "Social Studies for Citizens of a Strong and Free Nation," in *Social Curriculum Planning Resources* (Washington, D.C.: National Council for the Social Studies, 1990), 31-32.

Appendix C **ORGANIZATIONS DEVELOPING STANDARDS IN OTHER FIELDS OF STUDY**

For information on national standards in other fields of study, contact the following professional organizations:

The Arts
Music Educators National Conference
1806 Robert Fulton Drive
Reston, VA 20191
703-860-4000

Civics and Government
The Center for Civic Education
5146 Douglas Fir Road
Calabasas, CA 91302-1467
818-591-9321

Economics
The National Council on Economic
  Education
1140 Avenue of the Americas, 2nd Floor
New York, NY 10036
212-730-7007

English
The Center for the Study of Reading
University of Illinois
158 Children's Research Center
51 Gerty Drive
Champaign, IL 61820
217-333-2552

Foreign Language
American Council on the Teaching of
  Foreign Languages
Six Executive Plaza
Yonkers, NY 10801-6801
914-963-8830

Geography
National Council for Geographic Education
421 N. Walk, 16A Leonard Hall
Indiana University of Pennsylvania
Indiana, Pennsylvania 15705-1087
724-357-6290

Global Education
The American Forum for Global
  Education
120 Wall Street, 26th Floor
New York, NY 10005
212-624-1300

History
National Center for History
  in the Schools
Department of History
5262 Bunche Hall
University of California–Los Angeles
Los Angeles, CA 90095-1473
310-825-4702

Mathematics
National Council of Teachers of
  Mathematics
1906 Association Drive
Reston, VA 20191-1593
703-620-9840

Physical Education
National Association for Sport and
  Physical Education
1900 Association Drive
Reston, VA 20191
703-476-3410

Science
National Research Council
2101 Constitution Ave., NW
Washington, DC 20418
202-334-2000

Vocational Education
National Center for Research in
  Vocational Education
University of California, Berkeley
2030 Addison Street, Suite 500
Berkeley, CA 94720
510-642-4004

Supplement

A VISION OF POWERFUL TEACHING AND LEARNING IN THE SOCIAL STUDIES: BUILDING SOCIAL UNDERSTANDING AND CIVIC EFFICACY

This statement is a slightly revised version of the NCSS Position Statement "A Vision of Powerful Teaching and Learning in the Social Studies: Building Social Understanding and Civic Efficacy," which was prepared by the Task Force on Standards for Teaching and Learning in the Social Studies, and approved by the NCSS Board of Directors in 1992.

1. Background and Rationale
A. Introduction

These are challenging times for our nation's educators. As we approach the twenty-first century, renewal is in the air. Schools are experimenting with alternative organizational structures and educational practices. States and higher education institutions are reforming teacher education and professional development programs. Professional organizations are developing guidelines on content and methods to improve teaching.

The National Council for the Social Studies (NCSS) has contributed to these efforts by reaffirming citizen education as the primary purpose of social studies and by identifying the unique goals and essential characteristics of social studies programs designed to accomplish this purpose.

The NCSS House of Delegates voted overwhelmingly in November 1992 to approve the final version of the definition of "social studies" presented by the NCSS Board of Directors: "Social studies is the integrated study of the social sciences and humanities to promote civic competence. Within the school program, social studies provides coordinated, systematic study drawing upon such disciplines as anthropology, archaeology, economics, geography, history, law, philosophy, political science, psychology, religion, and sociology, as well as appropriate content from the humanities, mathematics, and the natural sciences. The primary purpose of the social studies is to help young people develop the ability to make informed and reasoned decisions for the public good as citizens of a culturally diverse, democratic society in an interdependent world."

NCSS recently issued position statements on curriculum, assessment, teacher education, and professional development. This document on teaching and learning complements those position statements by describing the forms of teacher-student discourse and the kinds of learning activities that can promote citizen education most effectively. Throughout the document, we use the word "powerful" to refer to those ideal forms of social studies teaching and learning.

Powerful social studies teaching helps students develop social understanding and civic efficacy. Social understanding is integrated knowledge of social aspects of the human condition: how they have evolved over time, the variations that occur in various physical environments and cultural settings, and the emerging trends that appear likely to shape the future. Civic efficacy—the readiness and willingness to assume citizenship responsibilities—is rooted in social studies knowledge and skills, along with related values (such as concern for the common good) and attitudes (such as an orientation toward participation in civic affairs). The nation depends on a well-informed and civic-minded citizenry to sustain its democratic traditions, especially now as it adjusts to its own heterogeneous society and its shifting roles in an increasingly interdependent and changing world.

1. Purpose of This Position Statement

This position statement sets forth a vision of social studies teaching and learning needed to produce the levels of social understanding and civic efficacy that the nation requires of its citizens. It also considers the teacher education programs and the community and governmental support for social studies needed to sustain such teaching and learning.

This document is broadly inclusive in its reference to "social studies." The term is intended to apply to all courses or units in social studies, social science, anthropology, civics, economics, geography, government, history, political science, psychology, sociology, and topics such as ethnic studies, global education, and law-related education. This position statement focuses, however, on what constitutes powerful teaching and learning within a unified social studies curriculum, and not on how much emphasis each content area should receive.

Consequently, this statement does not outline a K–12 social studies program or suggest any particular curricular scope and sequence. These and other content issues have been addressed by previous task forces and committees in *Social Studies Curriculum Planning Resources* (NCSS 1990). This position statement complements the documents in that collection by shifting the focus from content (what is taught) to method (how it is taught). Recognizing that teacher-student interaction is the heart of education, it offers guiding principles portraying ideal social studies teaching and learning. The principles have been synthesized by organizing findings from the best available classroom research around a core of ideas that represent an emerging consensus of expert opinion about how to teach social studies for understanding, appreciation, and life application.

The emphasis is on principles of teaching and learning that have enduring applicability across grade levels, content areas, and scope-and-sequence arrangements. These principles are summarized in the statement that social studies teaching and learning are powerful when they are meaningful, integrative, value-based, challenging, and active.

This vision statement summarizes these principles without presenting detailed elaboration, numerous examples, or discussion of related scholarly literature. A larger document currently in preparation will provide an annotated bibliography for readers who wish to pursue the scholarly basis for the principles and vignettes that illustrate their application in various K–12 social studies lessons and activities.

The focus of this document on teaching and learning processes is not intended to imply that such processes are goals in themselves or that curriculum planning should emphasize process over content. What is worth teaching well must be worth teaching, and there are many connections between worthwhile content and effective process. Ideal curriculum planning combines content and assessment components so that they complement one another and constitute coherent methods for accomplishing social studies goals.

In addition to displaying the characteristics described here, social studies teaching and learning must be subsumed within a coherent curricular scope and sequence. They also must be adapted to the topics and to the students taught at various grade levels. No attempt to address these complexities is made here, although some of them will be addressed in the forthcoming larger document.

Teaching and Learning

2. Intended Audience

This document has been written for social studies educators, educational policy-makers and administrators, publishers of educational materials, parents, and other interested parties. In particular, though, it is intended for teachers—the pivotal actors who shape the curriculum and effect change as they work with students. Articulating enduring principles that form a foundation for powerful teaching and learning, it is intended to advance social studies education as a profession, improve social studies teaching and teacher education, recognize and validate the effective practices that already exist in many classrooms, and provide a self-assessment tool for teachers.

3. Need for a Guiding Vision

There is a need for a guiding vision to assist social studies teachers in planning their instruction and focusing their students' learning. This need is derived from two features of social studies that distinguish it from other school subjects and provide special instructional challenges.

First, social studies is diverse, encompassing a great range of potential content. When taught well, its content is drawn not only from its most direct foundational disciplines but also from the arts and humanities, mathematics and science, current events, and students' own interests and experiences. This content, however, is not treated simply as collections of miscellaneous information and activities, but rather is organized within a coherent citizen education curriculum.

Second, the social understanding and civic efficacy goals of social studies place special responsibilities on teachers for addressing the ethical and social policy aspects of topics. When taught well, social studies engages students in the difficult process of confronting ethical and value-based dilemmas, and encourages students to speculate, think critically, and make personal and civic decisions based on information from multiple perspectives.

B. Social Studies Purposes and Goals

Powerful social studies teaching begins with a clear understanding of the subject's unique purposes and goals. NCSS's statement "Essentials of the Social Studies" (NCSS 1990, 9–11) identifies citizenship education as the primary purpose of K-12 social studies. Noting that concern for the common good and citizen participation in public life are essential to the health of our democratic system, it states that effective social studies programs prepare young people to identify, understand, and work to solve the problems facing our diverse nation in an increasingly interdependent world. Such programs:

- foster individual and cultural identity along with understanding of the forces that hold society together or pull it apart;
- include observation of and participation in the school and community;
- address critical issues and the world as it is;
- prepare students to make decisions based on democratic principles; and
- lead to citizen participation in public affairs.

Curriculum components include knowledge, democratic values and beliefs, thinking skills, and social and civic participation skills. Knowledge refers to interpretations that students construct in response to their experiences in and out of school. Knowledge is not merely a fixed body of information transmitted for students to memorize. Teachers should not only expose their students to curriculum content but should also provide them with opportunities to think and communicate in ways that will help students construct a working knowledge of such content.

The content of social studies focuses on the world—near and far, social and civic, past, present, and future. Effective social studies teaching draws this content from the social studies foundational disciplines (such as geography, government, and history) and links it with knowledge that students have acquired through life experiences and the media. It builds knowledge about the history and cultures of our nation and the world, geographical relationships, economic systems and processes, social and political institutions, interpersonal and intergroup relations, and worldwide relationships among nations, races, cultures, and institutions. From this knowledge base, exemplary programs help students to: (1) develop skills, concepts, and generalizations necessary to understand the sweep of human affairs: (2) appreciate the benefits of diversity and community, the value of widespread economic opportunity, and the contributions that people of both genders and the full range of ethnic, racial, and religious groups have made to our society; (3) become ready and willing to contribute to public policy formulation; and (4) acquire ways of managing conflict that are consistent with democratic procedures.

The fundamental values and beliefs taught in social studies are drawn from many sources, but especially from the Declaration of Independence and the United States Constitution with its Bill of Rights. These beliefs form the basic principles of our democratic constitutional order. They depend on such practices as due process, equal protection, free expression, and civic participation, and they have roots in the concepts of liberty, justice, equality, responsibility, diversity, and privacy. Exemplary programs do not indoctrinate students to accept these ideas blindly. Instead, they present knowledge about their historical derivation and contemporary application necessary to understand our society and its institutions. Teachers model fundamental democratic principles in their classrooms, discuss them as they relate to curriculum content and current events, and make them integral to the school's daily operations (e.g., through involving students in making decisions that affect them).

Exemplary social studies programs also prepare students to connect knowledge with beliefs and action using thinking skills that lead to rational behavior in social settings. These include the thinking skills involved in: (1) acquiring, organizing, interpreting, and communicating information; (2) processing data in order to investigate questions, develop knowledge, and draw conclusions; (3) generating and assessing alternative approaches to problems and making decisions that are both well informed and justified according to democratic principles; and (4) interacting with others in empathetic and responsible ways.

Teaching and Learning

Finally, exemplary social studies programs develop social and civic participation skills that prepare students to work effectively in diverse groups to address problems by discussing alternative strategies, making decisions, and taking action: to pursue social and civic agendas through persuasion, negotiation, and compromise; and to participate actively in civic affairs (e.g., by writing opinion letters to newspapers). Participation in informed public discussion of policy issues is direct preparation for active citizenship, especially when it culminates in decisions and actions that have real consequences.

The ideas set forth in the NCSS statement on the "Essentials of the Social Studies" are elaborated in its "Social Studies Curriculum Guidelines" (NCSS 1990, 12–15). The guidelines reaffirm that social studies teaching should draw from a broad range of content sources and use varied learning resources and activities. They also emphasize, however, that planning should be guided by basic and long-range social studies goals. Instruction should keep students aware of these goals, and assessments of teaching and learning should focus on the degree to which these goals have been accomplished.

Thus, a powerful social studies curriculum is unified by its purposes and goals. All of the components of such a curriculum—not only its content, but its instructional approaches, learning activities, and evaluation methods—are included in the curriculum because they are viewed as means for helping students acquire important capabilities and attitudes. By itself, the idea of cultural literacy construed in a narrow, name-recognition sense is not considered an adequate basis for content selection. Instead, content is included because it promotes progress toward major social understanding and civic efficacy goals, and it is taught accordingly. That is, instructional methods and activities should be planned to encourage students to connect what they are learning to their prior knowledge and experience, to think critically and creatively about what they are learning, and to use it in authentic application situations. Learning activities should be introduced and developed so as to make them minds-on activities that engage students with important ideas, not just hands-on activities that may or may not have educational value.

C. Assumptions About Social Studies as a School Subject

Several basic assumptions about the nature of social studies and its place in the school curriculum undergird the vision of powerful social studies presented in this position statement. These fundamental beliefs about social studies are assumed here as given.

1. Social studies is diverse. Social studies encompasses many more potential goals and content clusters than can be addressed adequately. Among both social studies teachers and the general public, there is disagreement about the relative importance of major social studies goals and content strands. Consequently, there never has been, and may never be, agreement on a single scope and sequence as the basis for a national social studies curriculum. Recognizing this, the NCSS curriculum guidelines state that goal setting and program development should be undertaken locally in response to locally perceived needs. To inform this process, NCSS has adopted a set of criteria for assessing scope-and-sequence plans and has endorsed three plans that meet these criteria as suitable for use as models by educational agencies and school districts (NCSS 1990,

17–70). *Locally developed curricula should reflect the essentials of the social studies and embody the principles in the NCSS curriculum guidelines, but their emphasis on goals and content strands can and should vary.*

The same assumption applies to the principles of powerful social studies teaching described here. This position statement does not attempt to prescribe ways to teach particular content because methods must be tailored to local needs. The statement does assume, however, that *both the content and the methods of instruction should be selected as means to accomplish major social understanding and civic efficacy goals.*

2. All students should have access to the full richness of the social studies curriculum. A complete core curriculum should be available to all students, not just gifted students in advanced programs. Tracking arrangements should not restrict important learning opportunities. In addition to acquiring basic knowledge and skills, all students at all grade levels should experience a social studies curriculum that includes ongoing engagement in thinking about social and civic problems and policy issues. This includes students at risk of school failure, students whose interests lie in other subject areas or vocational fields, and students who do not plan to attend college.

Special education students are often mainstreamed into social studies classes. This is as it should be, because all students need exposure to a diverse range of peers and opportunities to address social problems in group settings. Curricular planning for any special education students who are not mainstreamed should include full attention to social studies as well as to other subjects.

3. Teachers need adequate time and resources to teach social studies well at every grade level. The unique social understanding and civic efficacy goals of social studies will not be accomplished if it is treated as a collection of disconnected content to be covered as time allows. Social studies must be viewed as a basic K–12 curriculum component, and teachers and students must be supplied with materials and resources that reflect the students' needs and interests.

4. Social studies teachers need to treat the social world realistically and address its controversial aspects. To accomplish the major goals of this issue-oriented subject, teachers need both the freedom and the fortitude to address the real social world (not simply an idealized version) and to engage students in critical thinking about controversial topics. As they work to help students come to grips with social issues, teachers have both a responsibility to avoid inappropriate promotion of their personal views and a right to expect administrative and community support for their citizen education efforts.

II. A Vision of Powerful Social Studies Teaching and Learning

Informed by the major purposes and goals of social studies, the assumptions stated above, and the available research and scholarship, this position statement identifies key features of ideal social studies teaching and learning. These features are summed up in the statement that *social studies teaching and learning are powerful when they are meaningful, integrative, value-based, challenging, and active.*

These five key features are considered equally important. They are addressed in the

Teaching and Learning order presented here because such an order creates a natural flow of ideas, not because some key features are considered more essential than others.

A. Social Studies Teaching and Learning Are Powerful When They Are Meaningful

Powerful social studies teaching and learning are meaningful to both teachers and students. The content selected for emphasis is worth learning because it promotes progress toward important social understanding and civic efficacy goals, and teaching methods are designed to enable students to appreciate how the content relates to those goals. Rather than memorizing disconnected bits of information or practicing skills in isolation, *students learn connected networks of knowledge, skills, beliefs, and attitudes that they will find useful both in and outside of school.* This worthwhile content is taught in ways that relate to each student's culture and assists the student in recognizing its value. As a result, students' learning efforts are motivated by appreciation and interest, not just by accountability and grading systems. Students become disposed to care about what is happening in the world around them and to use the thinking frameworks and research skills of social science professionals to gather and interpret information. As a result, social learning becomes a lifelong interest and a basis for informed social action.

Thoughtfully planned to accomplish significant goals, meaningful social studies teaching embodies several other key features. *Instruction emphasizes depth of development of important ideas within appropriate breadth of topic coverage and focuses on teaching these important ideas for understanding, appreciation, and life application.* A great many facts, definitions, and generalizations are taught because understanding often-used information and ideas enhances communication within and between cultures. The most effective teachers, however, do not diffuse their efforts by covering too many topics superficially. Instead, they select for emphasis the most useful landmark locations, the most representative case studies, the most inspiring models, the truly precedent-setting events, and the concepts and principles that their students must know and be able to apply in their lives outside of school. Furthermore, teachers inform students of when and how this content will be useful to them in realistic contexts, and they follow through with activities that engage students in applying the content in simulated or real situations.

Facts and ideas are not taught in isolation from other content, nor are skills. Instead, they are embedded in *networks* of knowledge, skills, beliefs, and attitudes that are structured around important ideas and taught emphasizing their connections and potential applications.

The significance and meaningfulness of the content is emphasized both in how it is presented to students and how it is developed through activities. New topics are framed with reference to where they fit within the big picture, and students are alerted to their citizen education implications. The new content is developed in ways that help students see how its elements relate to one another (e.g., using diagrams of concept networks or causal chains, lists of key steps in narrative sequences, or other graphic learning aids or illustrations). Students are encouraged to process what they learn on several levels simultaneously, rather than always starting with low-level factual information and only later engaging in higher-order thinking. From the very beginning, students may be asked to relate new learning to prior knowledge, to think critically about it, or to use it to construct arguments or make informed decisions.

Teachers' questions are designed to promote understanding of important ideas and to stimulate thinking about their potential implications. As a result, *classroom interaction focuses on sustained examination of a few important topics rather than superficial coverage of many.* Teacher-student interactions emphasize thoughtful discussion of connected major themes, not rapid-fire recitation of miscellaneous bits of information.

Meaningful learning activities and assessment strategies focus students' attention on the most important ideas embedded in what they are learning. They encourage students to connect these ideas to their previous knowledge and experience, to think critically and creatively about them, and to consider their social implications. Thus, meaningful social studies teaching emphasizes *authentic activities and assessment tasks*—opportunities for students to engage in the sorts of applications of content that justify the inclusion of that content in the curriculum in the first place. For example, instead of labeling a map, students might plan a travel route and sketch landscapes that a traveler might see on the route. Instead of listing the amendments in the Bill of Rights, students might discuss or write about the implications of the Bill of Rights for a defendant in a selection of court cases. Instead of filling in a blank to complete the definition of a principle, students might use the principle to make predictions about a related situation or to guide their strategies in a simulation game.

This vision of meaningful social studies teaching and learning implies that the *teacher is reflective in planning, implementing, and assessing instruction.* Reflective teachers are well informed about the nature and purposes of social studies, and they remain current with developments in the field. They construct well-articulated ideas about their students' citizen education needs, plan their social studies teaching accordingly, and continue to adjust their practices in response to classroom feedback and growth in their own professional knowledge. They work within state and district guidelines, but adapt and supplement these guidelines and their adopted curriculum materials in ways that support their students' social studies education.

In particular, reflective teachers select and present content to students in ways that connect it with the students' interests and with local history, cultures, and issues. Local history and geography receive special attention, as do local examples of social, economic, political, or cultural topics studied at each grade level. There exists a systematic effort to increase awareness and validate the diversity found in the community by involving family members or local ethnic or cultural groups, encouraging students to share their cultural knowledge and experiences, and involving students in the community.

B. Social Studies Teaching and Learning Are Powerful When They Are Integrative

Social studies is naturally integrative because it addresses a broad range of content using varied instructional resources and learning activities. But powerful social studies

Teaching and
Learning

is both integrated and integrative in other respects as well.

First, *powerful social studies teaching is integrative in its treatment of topics.* It crosses disciplinary boundaries to address topics in ways that promote students' social understanding and civic efficacy. Its content is anchored by themes, generalizations, and concepts drawn from the social studies foundational disciplines, supplemented by ideas drawn from the arts, sciences, and humanities, from current events, and from local examples and students' experiences. Powerfully integrated social studies teaching builds a working knowledge of the evolution of the human condition through time, its current variations across locations and cultures, and an appreciation of the potential implications of this knowledge for social and civic decision-making.

Powerful social studies teaching is integrative across time and space, connecting with past experiences and looking ahead to the future. It helps students appreciate how aspects of the social world function, not only in their local community and in the contemporary United States but also in the past and in other cultures. It puts what is familiar to students into historical, geographical, and cultural perspectives, thus expanding their limited purviews on social phenomena that they may have taken for granted.

Powerful social studies teaching integrates knowledge, skills, beliefs, values, and attitudes to action. In particular, it teaches skills within the context of applying knowledge. Skills are included when they are necessary for applying content in natural ways. They are taught directly when opportunities for practice are embedded in authentic application activities. Content flow is not interrupted for practice of related skills.

Integrated social studies teaching and learning include effective use of technology that can add important dimensions to students' learning. Teachers can provide students with information through films, videotapes, videodiscs, and other electronic media, and they can teach students to use computers to compose, edit, and illustrate social studies research reports. Computer-based learning, especially games and simulations, can allow students to apply important ideas in authentic problem-tackling or decision-making contexts. If students have access to computerized data bases, they can search these resources for relevant research information. If they can communicate with peers in other states or nations, they can engage in personalized cultural exchanges or compare parallel data collected in geographically or culturally diverse locations.

Finally, *powerful social studies teaching integrates across the curriculum.* It provides opportunities for students to read and study text materials, appreciate art and literature, communicate orally and in writing, observe and take measurements, develop and display data, and in various other ways to conduct inquiry and synthesize findings using knowledge and skills taught in all school subjects. Because it addresses such a broad range of content and does so in an integrative fashion that includes attention to ethical and social policy implications, social studies is a natural bridging subject across the curriculum. Particularly in elementary and middle schools, instruction can feature social studies as the core around which the rest of the curriculum is built.

These integrative aspects have the potential for enhancing the scope and power of social studies. They also, however, have the potential for undermining its coherence and thrust as a curriculum component that addresses unique citizen education goals. A literary selection, writing assignment, cooperative learning activity, or computerized simulation cannot be considered curriculum simply because it features social studies combined with some other subject or set of skills. Nor can such activities be substituted for genuine social studies activities. To qualify as worthwhile elements of social studies curricula, activities must engage students in using important ideas in ways that promote progress toward social understanding and civic efficacy goals. Consequently, programs that feature a great deal of integration of social studies with other school subjects—even programs ostensibly built around social studies as the core of the curriculum—do not necessarily create powerful social studies learning. Unless they are developed as plans for accomplishing major social studies goals, such programs may focus on trivial or disconnected information.

C. Social Studies Teaching and Learning Are Powerful When They Are Value-Based

Powerful social studies teaching considers the ethical dimensions of topics and addresses controversial issues providing an arena for reflective development of concern for the common good and application of social values. Students learn to be respectful of the dignity and rights of others when interacting socially, and to emphasize basic democratic concepts and principles when making personal policy decisions or participating in civic affairs.

Topics are treated comprehensively and realistically, with attention to their disturbing or controversial aspects. *Students are made aware of potential social policy implications and taught to think critically and make value-based decisions about related social issues.* They learn to gather and analyze relevant information, assess the merits of competing arguments, and make reasoned decisions that include consideration of the values within alternative policy recommendations. Through discussions, debates, simulations, research, and other occasions for critical thinking and decision-making, students learn to apply value-based reasoning when addressing social problems.

The best social studies teachers develop awareness of their own values and how those values influence their selection of content, materials, questions, activities, and assessment methods. They assess their teaching from multiple perspectives and, where appropriate, adjust it to achieve a better balance.

Rather than promulgating personal, sectarian, or political views, these teachers make sure that students: (1) become aware of the values, complexities, and dilemmas involved in an issue; (2) consider the costs and benefits to various groups that are embedded in potential courses of action; and (3) develop well-reasoned positions consistent with basic democratic social and political values. The teacher provides guidance to such value-based reasoning especially when it is difficult to discern the connections between core democratic values and the issues at hand, when various core values suggest conflicting policies, or when there is conflict between these core values and students' personal or family values. When this is done most effectively, students may remain unsure about the teacher's personal views on an issue, at least until after it has been discussed thoroughly. Students become more aware of the complexities involved in addressing the issue in ways that serve the common good, and are more articulate about their own and others' policy recommendations and supporting rationales.

Powerful social studies teaching encourages recognition of opposing points of view, respect for well-supported positions, sensitivity to cultural similarities and differences, and a commitment to social responsibility and action. It recognizes the reality and persistence of tensions but promotes positive human relationships built on understanding, commitment to the common good, and willingness to compromise and search for common good.

D. Social Studies Teaching and Learning Are Powerful When They Are Challenging

Students are expected to strive to accomplish instructional goals both as individuals and as group members through thoughtful participation in lessons and activities and careful work on assignments. To establish a context that will support productively challenging teaching and learning, the teacher encourages the class to function as a learning community. Students learn that the purpose of reflective discussion is to work collaboratively to deepen understanding of the meanings and implications of content. Consequently, they are expected to listen carefully and respond thoughtfully to one another's ideas.

In advancing their own ideas and in responding critically to others, students are expected to build a case based on relevant evidence and arguments and to avoid derisive and other inappropriate behavior. They are challenged to come to grips with controversial issues, to participate assertively but respectfully in group discussions, and to work productively with partners or groups of peers in cooperative learning activities. Such experiences foster the development of competencies essential to civic efficacy.

Making social studies teaching challenging should not be construed as merely articulating high standards and then leaving it to students to try to meet them. Rather, *the teacher models seriousness of purpose and a thoughtful approach to inquiry and uses instructional strategies designed to elicit and support similar qualities from students.* The teacher paves the way for successful learning experiences by making sure that the content is suited to the students' developmental levels and cultural backgrounds and by providing assistance that enables students to handle challenging activities. The teacher also makes it clear, however, that students are expected to connect thoughtfully what they are learning to their prior knowledge and experience, to offer comments, and to raise questions.

To stimulate and challenge students' thinking, teachers should expose them to many information sources that include varying perspectives on topics and offer conflicting opinions on controversial issues. Questions call for thoughtful examination of the content, not just retrieval of information from memory. After posing such questions, the teacher allows sufficient time for students to think and formulate responses and to elaborate on their peers' responses.

Many of the questions call for critical or creative thinking, suggested solutions to problems, or reasoned positions on policy issues. Such questions often produce numerous and conflicting responses. When this occurs, the teacher withholds evaluation and instead invites the students to engage in sustained dialogue and debate. This shifts some of the authority for evaluating the validity of knowledge from teacher to students.

Challenge is also communicated in the teacher's reactions to students' ideas. The teacher shows interest in and respect for students' thinking, but demands well-reasoned arguments rather than opinions voiced without adequate thought or commitment. Routinely, students are asked to explain and defend their ideas using content-based arguments. Instead of always accepting students' views or asking the class to discuss them, the teacher sometimes challenges students' assumptions or responds with comments or questions that help students identify misconceptions, flaws in the argument, or unrecognized complications. The teacher must act with sensitivity, because some students become anxious or embarrassed when someone questions their ideas in this way. The teacher makes it clear that the purpose of such a challenge is not to put students on the spot but to help them construct new understanding through engagement in thoughtful dialogue.

E. Social Studies Teaching and Learning Are Powerful When They Are Active

Powerful social studies teaching and learning are rewarding, but they demand a great deal from both teachers and students. Thoughtful preparation and instruction by the teacher and sustained effort by students are required for students to make sense of and apply what they are learning.

Powerful social studies teaching demands that the teacher actively make curricular plans and adjustments. Rather than mechanically following the instructions in a manual, an exemplary teacher is prepared to: (1) acquire and update continuously the subject-matter knowledge and related pedagogical knowledge needed to teach the content effectively; (2) adjust goals and content to the students' needs; (3) participate as a partner in learning with students, modeling the joy of both discovering new knowledge and increasing understanding of familiar topics; (4) use a variety of instructional materials such as physical examples, photographs, maps, illustrations, films, videos, textbooks, literary selections, and computerized databases; (5) plan field trips, visits to the class by resource people, and other experiences that will help students relate what they are learning to their lives outside the classroom; (6) plan lessons and activities that introduce content to students, and encourage them to process it actively, think about it critically and creatively, and explore its implications; (7) develop current or local examples that relate the content to students' lives; (8) plan sequences of questions that allow for numerous responses and stimulate reflective discussion; (9) provide students with guidance and assistance as needed, yet encourage them to assume increasing responsibility for managing their own learning; (10) structure learning environments and activities in ways that encourage students to behave as a community of learners; (11) use accountability and grading systems that are compatible with instructional methods and that focus on accomplishment of major social understanding and civic efficacy goals; and (12) monitor reflectively and adjust as necessary.

Besides advance planning and preparation, *active social studies teaching requires reflective thinking and decision-making as events unfold during instruction.* Teachers must adjust plans to developing circumstances such as teachable moments that arise when students ask questions, make comments, or offer challenges worth pursuing. The teacher decides whether to persist with a topic or conclude it and move on to a new topic, whether to try to elicit an insight from students or to supply it directly, and how thoroughly the students will need to be prepared for an activity before they can begin work on it independently.

After the teacher launches an activity and students are working on their own or in collaboration with their peers, the teacher remains active by monitoring individual or group progress and providing assistance. Interventions are designed to clear up confusion, while enabling students to cope with task demands productively; students should be allowed to handle as much of the task as they can at the moment while at the same time making progress toward fully independent and successful performance. The teacher does not perform the tasks for students or simplify them to the point that they no longer engage the students in the cognitive processes required to accomplish the activity's goals.

Students develop new understanding through a process of active construction. They do not passively receive or copy curriculum content; rather, they actively process it by relating it to what they already know (or think they know) about the topic. Instead of relying on rote learning methods, they strive to make sense of what they are learning by developing a network of connections that link the new content to preexisting knowledge and beliefs anchored in their prior experience. Sometimes the learning involves conceptual change in which students discover that some of their beliefs are inaccurate and need to be modified.

The construction of meaning required to develop important social understanding takes time and is facilitated by interactive discourse. Clear explanation and modeling from the teacher are important, as are opportunities to answer questions about content, discuss or debate the meanings and implications of content, or use the content in activities that call for tackling problems or making decisions. These activities allow students to process content actively and make it their own by paraphrasing it into their own words, exploring its relationship to other knowledge and to past experience, appreciating the insights it provides, or identifying its implications for social or civic decision-making.

Teacher and student roles shift as learning progresses. Early in a unit of study, the teacher may need to provide considerable guidance by modeling, explaining, or supplying information that builds on students' existing knowledge while also assuming much of the responsibility for structuring and managing learning activities. As students develop expertise, however, they can begin to assume responsibility for regulating their learning by asking questions and by working on increasingly complex applications with increasing degrees of autonomy. The teacher still assists students with challenges they are not yet ready to handle by themselves but such assistance is gradually reduced in response to increases in students' readiness to engage in independent and self-regulating learning.

Because what one learns is intimately linked to how one learns it, powerful social studies programs feature learning that is both social and active. The learning is social because it occurs in a group setting and includes substantial student-student interaction during discussions and collaborative work on activities. The learning is active because the curriculum emphasizes hands-on (and minds-on) activities that call for students to react to what they are learning and use it for some authentic purpose.

Effective activities encourage students to think about and apply what they are learning. Teachers may provide opportunities for students to apply their existing knowledge to questions about new content, to understand new content, to synthesize and communicate what they have learned, to generate new knowledge or make creative applications, or to think critically about the content and make decisions or take actions that relate to it.

Powerful social studies teaching emphasizes authentic activities that call for using content for accomplishing life applications. For example, critical-thinking attitudes and abilities are developed through policy debates or assignments calling for critique of currently or historically important policy arguments or decisions, not through artificial exercises in identifying logical or rhetorical flaws. Similarly, in addition to more traditional assignments, students frequently engage in cooperative learning, construction of models or plans, dramatic re-creations of historical events that shaped democratic values or civic policies, role-play, and simulation activities (e.g., mock trials or simulated legislative activities, interviewing family members, and collecting data in the local community). They also participate in various social and civic roles (e.g., discussing home safety or energy conservation checklists with parents and planning appropriate follow-up action, participating in student government activities and local community restoration or improvement efforts, or doing volunteer work for nursing homes or political campaigns).

Through such activities, students develop social understanding that they can explain in their own words and can access and apply in appropriate situations. For example, they learn to think critically as they read newspapers and magazines, watch television, or monitor political or policy debates. They learn to recognize the problematic aspects of statements, to project the probable social consequences of advocated policies, and to take these complexities into account when forming their opinions.

The teacher's modeling, classroom management, motivational techniques, instructional methods, and assessment procedures all communicate to students that they are expected to participate in social studies classes actively and with a sense of purpose. The students learn to reflect thoughtfully on what they are learning and to ask questions, share opinions, and engage in public content-based dialogue. Through authentic application activities they develop civic efficacy by practicing it—engaging in the inquiry and debate required to make informed decisions about real social issues then following up with appropriate social or civic action.

III. Making It Happen:
Developing and Maintaining Powerful Social Studies Programs

The kind of powerful social studies teaching and learning envisioned here is realized most fully when it is encouraged and reinforced by other components of the educational system. In particular, powerful social studies teaching and learning are likely to become more common to the extent that: (1) assessment approaches at all levels focus on measuring progress toward social understanding and efficacy goals; (2) teachers benefit from effective preservice preparation and in-service professional development programs, and social studies education receives support from school administrators, parents, the local community, and government agencies; and (3) the nation successfully meets certain currently recognizable challenges, including the need for additional research on powerful social studies teaching and learning, for improvements in curriculum materials and technologies, and for improvement efforts that focus on accomplishing our most important educational goals. These systemic influences on social studies education are addressed in the following sections.

A. Assessment of Social Studies Teaching and Learning

Powerful social studies teaching and learning include assessment components designed to inform instructional planning and thus produce continuing improvements through successive cycles. The assessment mechanisms focus on the degree to which major social understanding and civic efficacy goals are accomplished, rather than on measuring acquisition of miscellaneous information or command of generic skills. Care is taken to see that testing does not place inappropriate content coverage pressures on teachers or cause them to shift their emphasis away from pursuing major social studies goals.

The NCSS curriculum guidelines (1990) call for systematic and rigorous assessment of social studies instruction that is based primarily on each school's stated objectives as the criteria for effectiveness. Knowledge, thinking skills, valuing, and social participation are assessed, using data from many sources in addition to paper-and-pencil tests. These data provide a basis for planning curriculum improvements as well as for assessing students' learning. The guidelines emphasize locally planned assessment of progress toward locally established goals.

In 1991, NCSS elaborated on these guidelines through a position statement on testing and evaluation of social studies students. This statement calls for transforming student assessment from an overreliance on machine-scored standardized tests to approaches that balance such measures with more authentic performance assessments. These include tasks such as speaking effectively or articulating a reasoned stance on a controversial social issue. Such assessments focus on the processes that students use, not merely on the answers they choose.

A comprehensive assessment plan for social studies includes daily monitoring of the general effectiveness and quality of student participation in lessons and activities, as well as appropriate use of both criterion- and norm-referenced tests. The primary purpose of testing should be to improve teaching and learning. To accomplish this purpose, teachers need the freedom and encouragement to select or develop assessment tasks that are suited to their students and aligned with locally adopted social studies goals. This process will involve augmenting traditional tests with performance evaluations, portfolios of student papers and projects, and essays focusing on higher-order thinking and applications. The assessment devices must be fair to all students and interpreted with sensitivity to the propriety of any norms or comparison groups that might be used to place the scores of local students into context. Teachers must have access to all data collected in their classrooms and be proficient in interpreting and reporting results.

A basic underlying principle is that assessment should be aligned with, and designed to help accomplish, the citizen education goals that drive the social studies curriculum. The curriculum's assessment component should not drive its content and process components; instead, all three components should constitute a coherent plan for accomplishing the curriculum's major social understanding and civic efficacy goals. To the extent that the assessment component creates content or skills coverage pressures that do not promote significant progress toward these goals, it is counterproductive to the purposes of social studies. The same may be true of test-driven coverage pressures in other subject areas if these pressures result in inadequate time allocations to social studies or loss of its coherence as an integral curriculum component.

B. Support for Powerful Social Studies Teaching and Learning

If social studies teaching and learning are to begin to approximate the vision outlined here, more support for social studies education at every level is necessary. Such support includes internal support from the profession itself (emphasizing improvements in preservice and in-service teacher education) and external support from parents, the local community, and government agencies.

1. Preparing Preservice Teachers

In 1987, NCSS developed a position statement and guidelines on the preparation of social studies teachers. The guidelines refer to admission and continuation of students in teacher education programs, characteristics of these programs, and characteristics of the sponsoring institutions. Social studies professionals should lobby for state staffing policies that reflect the NCSS teacher preparation standards.

Academic and continuation requirements should ensure that candidates possess sufficient knowledge and skills, as well as appropriate personal and ethical qualities. Programs should include: (1) general education preparation in the humanities, the social and behavioral sciences, the natural sciences, mathematics, and computer science; (2) special emphasis on foundational disciplines for the social studies, approached within a global perspective and with attention to value conflicts and policy issues; and (3) a professional education component that includes courses in social and philosophical foundations, human growth and development, psychology of learning, needs of exceptional students, gender and ethnic perspectives, use of media, and a range of planning, teaching, and assessment skills.

Social studies methods courses should prepare prospective teachers to select, integrate, and translate knowledge and methodology from the social studies into curricula suitable for the grade levels at which they expect to teach. Programs should include both information and clinical experiences designed to prepare prospective teachers to teach social studies in a variety of settings to a variety of students using a variety of approaches to curriculum, instruction, and assessment. Student teaching experiences should span complete school semesters, not just college quarters, and they should be supervised by appropriately qualified cooperating teachers and college or university personnel.

Institutions sponsoring teacher education programs should vest responsibility for managing those programs in the head of the college, school, or department of education and should staff the program with faculty members who have experience in K–12 schools. These faculty members should excel as teachers or field supervisors, not just as scholars. They should observe and interact with their student teachers in school settings often enough to assess the student teachers' progress accurately and to model or suggest improvements adapted to the settings.

Effective preparation of social studies teachers requires close cooperation between the social science specialists and the teacher education specialists, as well as between the university personnel and school personnel involved in clinical and field experiences. *All of the participants in teacher education programs should understand and be committed to major social studies goals, should be knowledgeable about powerful social studies teaching, and should model such teaching in their classrooms.* This implies use of a broad range of teaching and learning methods. Prospective teachers need coaching and structured opportunities to develop their skills at using approaches such as lecture and discussion, cooperative learning, panel discussions, debates, games, simulations, community participation experiences, and computerized data bases and learning programs. Besides learning the procedural aspects of these varied approaches, prospective teachers should learn to shift their managerial and instructional roles appropriately and to prepare students to assume additional responsibilities for managing their learning. Teachers need to function comfortably not just as experts but also as guides.

Learning to plan, implement, and assess powerful social studies teaching on a consistent basis will require years of guided in-service and self-assessment experiences in addition to good preservice preparation. At a minimum, however, preservice programs should equip new teachers with a basic understanding of social studies purposes and goals and a vision of powerful social studies teaching and learning that they can use to guide their subsequent professional development.

2. Supporting In-Service Teachers

The vision of powerful social studies teaching and learning outlined here assumes local planning and decision-making in which teams of teachers identify and clarify goals, plan the social studies program, monitor it reflectively, and make necessary adjustments. To make this possible, school districts and building administrators need to allocate sufficient in-class time for social studies teaching and provide sufficient out-of-class time for collegial planning and professional development. Although social studies is rich in opportunities for connecting content from other subjects, it features important purposes and goals of its own and must be taught with frequency and coherence for these goals to be accomplished. Throughout grades K–12, all students should receive daily instruction in a carefully planned social studies program.

Teaching staffs need collegial planning time and in-service staff development activities to ensure that all teachers develop a shared understanding of the broad goals of social studies education and thus approach them with an emphasis on building social understanding and civic efficacy. Guided by these major goals and a knowledgeable social studies coordinator, collegial planning should yield a coherent social studies program for the entire school. All teachers should know what their colleagues are doing and understand how the components assigned to their grade level fit into the big picture. Planning should be guided by the NCSS collection of curriculum planning resources (1990) and should incorporate the instructional principles outlined in this position statement. The program should include an assessment component that aligns with goals and complements the other program components (the value and attitudinal aspects as well as the knowledge and skills aspects).

Teachers need support for acquiring and receiving social studies information, resources, and teaching and assessment strategies. All teachers need opportunities to obtain information about and assistance in using social studies resources from competent consultants, opportunities to visit other classrooms to see demonstrations of powerful teaching and learning, and involvement in decision-making concerning adoption of curriculum materials or other changes in the school's social studies program. New teachers need mentoring from accomplished teachers. Teachers with special interests or assignments need release time and support for attendance at state and national conferences, activity in professional organizations, local networking, and the opportunity to help develop curriculum materials or program plans. Teachers should be encouraged to identify their group and individual professional development needs relating to social studies, and arrangements should be made to address these needs.

Experienced teachers interested in doing so may apply for assessment and NCSS advanced professional certification of the quality of their social studies teaching (NCSS 1991). Whether or not they seek council certification in addition to their state certification, however, teachers who have continuing responsibility for social studies education should strive to meet NCSS's standards for certified professionals. In particular, they should: (1) continue their professional development through formal course work, attendance at conferences, professional reading, and collaboration with peers on action research or staff development projects; (2) analyze their and their students' work products; (3) keep a journal on practice; and (4) take active roles in professional and community organizations.

Social studies education should receive vigorous support as a vital curriculum component responsible for accomplishing uniquely important purposes and goals. A social studies coordinator should be appointed for the district as a whole and for each building. The district should provide appropriate instructional time, materials and resources, facilities, and equipment for all teachers. They will need access to carefully selected textbooks and the many types of data sources that are used in powerful social studies teaching, including auxiliary texts, multimedia kits, reference materials and text supplements at various reading levels, maps, globes, physical artifacts, films and tapes, computer equipment and software, content-correlated literature selections, and equipment for simulations or special events.

Districts should encourage their social studies teachers to participate in active curriculum committees that have decision-making as well as advisory responsibilities. Finally, a district-wide policy statement on academic freedom and responsibility should be in place. Social studies teachers should be able to rely on this statement and on administrative support for their efforts to model civic participation and assist their students to confront social issues.

3. External Support from Communities and Governments

Several forms of community and governmental support will be required to sustain powerful social studies programs. Most fundamentally, communities and governments need to recognize the subject's vital purpose for citizen education and thus prepare to support accomplishment of its social understanding and civic efficacy goals and the powerful forms of teaching and learning necessary to accomplish them. This commitment implies sustaining teacher education and professional development programs and forms of support for social studies in schools as described in previous sections. These aspects of powerful social studies programs require funding and leadership support from local school districts and state governments.

Corporate and business interests can be supportive as well. Sponsoring cooperative programs, hosting field trips, supplying guest speakers, and supporting local heritage preservations that serve as school resources are just some of the ways local businesses and communities can support their schools' social studies programs. Parents can help by donating or lending cultural or historical artifacts, acting as chaperones on field trips, and visiting classes or resource people (e.g., to provide information about their occupations or their ethnic heritages).

C. The Challenges for the Future

The vision of powerful social studies teaching and learning set forth here has been informed by a growing knowledge base about the ingredients for teaching social studies for understanding, appreciation, and life application. This position statement, however, is just a beginning. The future holds many challenges that must be met if the vision of powerful social studies teaching and learning outlined here is to be developed in more detail and become the basis for standard practice in the schools.

More research on social studies teaching and learning is needed, especially research that focuses on teachers' efforts to develop social understanding and civic efficacy in their students. Studies that document the effects of powerful social studies teaching and describe it in detail as it unfolds across a lesson or curriculum unit would be especially valuable. Also needed are studies of what students at the various grade levels know (or think they

know) about the content taught in those grades and how instruction affects their thinking. This information then can be used to develop ways to adapt instruction so as to
build on students' valid knowledge and address their misconceptions.

As the knowledge base develops, it will need to consider the situational characteristics of various teaching contexts. The general principle that social studies teaching and
learning become more powerful when they are meaningful, integrative, value-based,
challenging, and active applies to all social studies classes, but the specifics involved in
bringing this principle to life will vary according to individual students and content
areas. More information is needed about the particular forms of powerful social studies
teaching that best suit various grade levels and content areas, how to adapt these forms
of instruction to meet the needs of diverse learners, and what constitutes effective pre-
service and in-service social studies teacher education.

*Improved learning resources, along with research on how to use them effectively, are also
needed.* Textbooks need to be structured coherently around powerful ideas developed in
depth, and they need to be supplemented with a wide range of learning resources and
activities. In the early elementary grades, multimedia kits, picture books, simplified
maps, collections of artifacts (or realistic reproductions), and other instructional tools
and data sources designed for students who have not yet become sophisticated readers
are needed. Across the grades, computerized data bases, simulations, and games,
laserdiscs, hypermedia, scanners, electronic mail connections with classrooms in other
states or nations, and production and use of videotapes as teaching and learning devices
have potential for social studies applications. These applications will need to be developed and studied to determine how to make the best use of their unique capabilities in
the most cost-effective ways. Research and development also need to attend to the
changes in the teacher's role entailed in many of these innovations. Along with access
to new resources and technologies, teachers will need guidance on how to manage these
multiple resources and help their students learn to use them more effectively.

Certain systematic changes in education in the United States are needed to support
fully powerful social studies teaching and learning. Most of these are changes that
would improve the quality of instruction across the curriculum. Critics of textbooks
and learning resources in all subjects are voicing similar concerns about the need to shift
emphasis from breadth of coverage to depth of development of important content, to
shift from fill-in-the-blank worksheets to a broader range of activities, and to replace
tests that create counterproductive content coverage pressures with authentic, varied,
and goals-driven assessment components. School restructuring efforts have stressed
teacher empowerment and collegial planning, although more emphasis should be
placed on articulating major goals and on developing local networks of teachers who
share similar teaching assignments.

Some of the current assessment reform movements are encouraging, especially
those calling for authentic tasks. If these efforts are to support powerful teaching and
learning, however, test users will have to be willing to accept the costs of authentic
assessment. Also, social studies assessments will have to shift from a focus on generic

Teaching and Learning skills to a focus on social understanding and civic efficacy goals, including those relating to the teaching of democratic values.

IV. Summary

Complementing position statements on social studies curriculum, evaluation, teacher preparation, and advanced certification published previously by the National Council for the Social Studies, this position statement sets forth a vision of powerful social studies teaching and learning needed to accomplish important social understanding and civic efficacy goals. It briefly considers assessment approaches that will complement powerful social studies teaching and learning; preservice teacher preparation programs, in-service professional development programs, and forms of support for social studies education in the schools that are necessary to sustain such powerful teaching and learning; and some needed developments in research, instructional resources, and educational reform. In putting forth a vision of the ideal, this position statement emphasizes that social studies teaching and learning become powerful when they are meaningful, integrative, value-based, challenging, and active.

V. Conclusion

Thomas Jefferson, among others, emphasized that the vitality of a democracy depends upon the education and participation of its citizens. If the nation is to develop fully the readiness of its citizenry to carry forward its democratic traditions, it will need to support progress toward full attainment of the vision of powerful social studies teaching and learning outlined here.

References

National Council for the Social Studies. "Standards for the Preparation of Social Studies Teachers." Washington, D.C.: National Council for the Social Studies, 1987.

————. "Social Studies Curriculum Planning Resources." Washington, D.C.: National Council for the Social Studies, 1990.

————. Application for Advanced Certification for Teachers of Social Studies. Washington, D.C.: National Council for the Social Studies, 1991.

————. "Testing and Evaluation of Social Studies Students." *Social Education* 55 (September 1991): 284-86.

Task Force on Standards for Teaching and Learning in the Social Studies

Margit McGuire, *Co-chair, Seattle University, Seattle, Washington*

James F. Marran, *Co-chair, New Trier High School, Winnetka, Illinois*

Silvia Alvarez, *Albuquerque Public Schools, Albuquerque, New Mexico*

Susan Austin, *Bala Cynwyd, Pennsylvania*

Jere Brophy, *Michigan State University, East Lansing, Michigan*

George Mehaffy, *San Diego State University, San Diego, California*

Pat Nickell, *Fayette County Schools, Lexington, Kentucky*

Linda Preston, *Burlington, Massachusetts*

Michael Young, *Elkhorn, Nebraska*

Responses to the statement on powerful teaching and learning in the social studies were received from:

James Akenson	Michael Hartoonian
Virginia Atwood	M. Gail Hickey
Buckley Barnes	Kristi Karis
Allan Brandhorst	Lillian Katz
Jean Claugus	Linda Levstik
Paul Cohen	Tedd Levy
O. L. Davis	Peter Martorella
James Donlevy	Mindy McMahon
Jean Fair	Jack Morgan
Darlene Fisher	Isidore Starr
Ann Fleener	Tina Thuermer
Jackie Fuller	Mary Jane Turner
Jim Garretson	Huber Walsh
Jeanette Groth	Leo West
Teri Harper